HEALING NOW

ALSO BY FERRAN BLASCO-AGUASCA

Where Heaven and Earth Unite
(Written with Elyn Aviva)

HEALING NOW

A PATH TO OPTIMAL WELL-BEING AND SELF-LOVE

THROUGH HEALING MEDITATION

Ferran Blasco-Aguasca

Joyful Heart Institute Publications
Shen Dao LLC
Rochester, Michigan
2020

MEDICAL DISCLAIMER

This book is not a substitute for the medical advice of a physician or medical treatment. Before participating in any of the exercises from this book, the reader is strongly recommended to consult with a physician or other healthcare provider. The reader should also regularly consult a physician in matters relating to his/her health, particularly with respect to any symptoms that may require diagnosis or medical attention.

Joyful Heart Institute Publications – Shen Dao LLC
126 East 3rd Street
Rochester, Michigan 48307 USA
www.joyfulheartinstitute.com

The information provided in this book is correct to the best of the author's knowledge and ability; however, there may be errors of interpretation or understanding. Links to the Internet were accurate at the time of publication but may change from time to time. For this reason, hot links may no longer be functioning.

ISBN (Print edition): 978-1-081739645
Library of Congress Control Number: 2019911231

"Don't run, go slowly,
It is only to yourself that you have to go!
Go slowly, don't run,
For the child of yourself, just born and eternal
Cannot follow you."

~Juan Ramón Jiménez
(*Eternidades*, 1916)

CONTENTS

ACKNOWLEDGMENTS

I want to express my deepest gratitude to my teachers and mentors in the field of healing meditation:

Juan Li, Howard Lee, Bernie and Marisol Bayard, Juan Sáez, and Adriano Angelo who introduced me to the traditions of Taoist healing meditation and five elements inner alchemy.

Master Hua Ching Ni and his two sons, Daoshing Ni and Maoshing Ni, from whom I learned Chinese Medicine, acupuncture, and Taoist cosmology at Yo San University.

Sifu Franklin Fick, from whom I learned Tai Chi, Qi Gong, and the basis for the *Dry Bath* self-massage that comprises chapter four of this book.

Garchen Rinpoche, Chokyi Nyima Rinpoche, Khenchen Tsewang Gyatso, Lama Pema Chopel, Namkhai Norbu, Tenzin Wyangal, Tulku Sherdor, Tulku Dragmar, Khenpo Samdup, and Dr. Nida Chenagtsang from whom I learned the foundations of Buddhist yoga and philosophy.

Tracy Flynn and Hojoung Audenaerde, from whom I learned ashtanga and restorative yoga.

Esther Hicks and Abraham, who helped deepen my understanding of what healing and well-being are.

Dr. Mark Dyczkowski, whose friendship, love, and wisdom are a constant source of joy, support, and inspiration for me. It was a conversation with him about the nature of breathing that inspired this book.

I also want to express my deepest gratitude to Dr. Jim Quinn for his heartfelt companionship and his generous, thorough, and insightful guidance during all the stages of this project; to Beatriz Blasco and Luke Gerwe for reviewing and formatting the manuscript; to Honora Wolfe for painting the art for the cover; to Irene Blasco, Christian Martínez and Josh Wallace for their contributions to the line drawings; to Yan Blasco Ivanov for shooting and editing the photographs that illustrate the practices; and to Diane Adair, John Aldwardt, Elyn Aviva, Missie Nordrum, Caryl Phillips, and Lotte Sangstad, for their insights and wise advice to make this book better.

Finally, my most sincere gratitude to my parents, Sylvia and Carmelo, to my wife, Brooke, and to all the students who since 2002 have participated in the retreats and classes I have led. In their unique ways, they have taught me that joy, love, and kindness are the greatest healers.

THE PRACTICE OF HEALING MEDITATION

Healing is an expression of love. The greater our love towards others, the world, and ourselves, the more well-being and happiness we experience. This love though is not the common worldly love, where good intentions are mixed with hope, fear, attachment, and jealousy. The love that heals arises out of the recognition—or at least the theoretical understanding—of our divine and perfectly pure nature.

Love heals because its warmth reminds us that our essential nature is free and open, like a boundless, clear sky. From our heart—the sun in that cloudless sky—blissful sunrays of love and well-being shine in all directions. Unimpeded, these sunrays radiate through our actions, words, and thoughts, filling up the infinite vastness of our being with generosity, kindness, joy, compassion, patience, optimism, and many other virtues. As these sunrays extend into our life, our relationships, and the world at large, we feel well, happy, and abundant.

But it often happens, sometimes for long periods of time, that we get distracted from our essential nature. When we are distracted from who we are, emotions such as numbness, fear, anger, hatred, attachment, and jealousy form as clouds that appear in the sky. These clouds temporarily block our natural inner radiance. Even though the sunrays—our love and well-being—never disappear, when the clouds cover the sky of our being for long enough, we forget that the sun still shines behind the clouds. Not only that, we also forget that we are the sky. Instead, we start believing that we are the clouds. Then we feel physically, energetically, emotionally, and mentally ill.

What Is Healing Meditation?

Healing meditation is a system of practices that invites us to remember the vastness of who we are by encouraging us to focus on the sunrays instead of the clouds. Even if we might feel ill and our body might be going through an illness process, healing meditation guides us to realize that our love, joy, and well-being have never left us. Even in the darkest and cloudiest situation, love, joy, and well-being remain as our boundless and flawless essence, the wonder of wonders.

By inspiring us to renew our view of life, healing meditation guides us to reawaken well-being in our body, positive emotions in our heart, insight in our mind, and clarity in our consciousness. Through healing meditation, by sustaining our attention on life's joyful radiance, we soften and dispel the clouds—the anger, grudges, resentment, and fear—that separate us from others and ourselves. As the sunrays from our heart shine with more ease and openness, reaching further inside and outside us, the clouds thin and dissolve. Then magic happens: we remember who we are and what the world is, and we heal.

The deepest power of healing meditation comes from transforming our mind and emotions. This is so because our thinking, our points of view, and our idea of what is possible determine how we feel and how we heal. While we all want well-being and happiness, often instead we think and talk about the clouds that cover the sky of our being. By continuously ruminating and telling others and ourselves about our problems, illnesses, and pains, we perpetuate them.

Focusing on what we don't want, even if done with good intent, we thicken the layer of clouds that cover our inner sky. Wanting well-being while constantly referring to its absence in our life is like trying to drive a car with one foot on the gas pedal and the other foot on the brake pedal. We could sit there for thirty years and still not move one inch.

Through the practice of healing meditation, we realize that

our experience of reality reflects our thought patterns and personal vibration. This realization encourages us to overcome the habit of reinforcing physical and mental gloom, even when our mind could justify plenty of reasons to despair. Instead, healing meditation brings out the best from within us by encouraging us to search for the best possible thoughts and to feel the joy of the best possible outcomes. Through repeated practice, we become accustomed to sustaining a healthy vision of ourselves and our world, a vision that heals because it aligns us with our most intimate desire for well-being, happiness, and joy.

During healing meditation practice, we consciously choose how we want our body and mind to feel. Based on the premise that kind thoughts and self-love increase well-being, we cultivate an image of ourselves as being radiant with health and clarity. As we sustain this image through practice, we transform how we see ourselves, and this new image becomes the foundation of our daily experience.

Healing meditation invites us to reflect on what kinds of thoughts we entertain from moment to moment. It asks us to examine, in this moment, "Who is making my decisions for me? Am I giving my personal power away to old habits? To family patterns? To past traumas? To the media?" Calling us to discern where we can regain energetic integrity—our ability to maintain our energy systems in an optimal state that supports our physical, emotional, and mental well-being—healing meditation guides us to become the heartful owners of our own life. As our practice empowers us with greater self-confidence, we joyfully embrace ourselves for the miracle that we truly are.

From the simplicity of observing our breath to the richness of harmonizing the universal elements within, healing meditation also allows us to see that our inner divine nature is the source of healing and well-being. Through healing meditation, we learn to embrace this essential divine nature, letting it shine as the sun shines in the clear sky for our benefit and the benefit of all those around us.

Benefits of Practicing Healing Meditation

As human beings, we live our life through three fundamental layers of experience: matter (our physical body), energy (our sensations and emotions), and mind-spirit (our thoughts and perceptions). When these three layers are in harmony, our body feels well, we have the vitality to do what we want to do, and our spirit stays centered, calm, and kind.

However, in our fast-paced world, disconnected from nature and dependent on technology, these three layers and the inner elements associated with them easily fall out of balance. When any aspect of our body, energy, or mind-spirit is not functioning properly, or when the relationship among these three layers is disrupted, we lose our inner alignment. When this happens, we experience energetic dispersion and fragmentation. If not corrected, this temporary situation leads to various symptoms and illnesses: from physical challenges such as body pain, digestive complications, hormonal imbalances, low immunity, and fatigue, to mental-emotional challenges such as stress, anxiety, insomnia, lack of motivation, and feelings of unclear purpose in life. Regardless of how different from each other all these symptoms and illnesses might seem, at the root of all these challenges we find an inner disconnect between our body, our energy, and our mind.

Through the alignment of our posture, our breathing and our intention, healing meditation guides us to regain and maintain a harmonious relationship between our physical body, our energetic system, and our mental-spiritual essence. This renewed inner harmony helps us by:

- Reducing stress, increasing relaxation, and balancing our nervous system.
- Improving our breathing, promoting better blood circulation, and balancing blood pressure.
- Promoting better digestion, absorption of nutrients, and elimination of toxins.

- Improving sleep and maintaining good energy levels.
- Strengthening our immunity and reducing the length of acute illness.
- Promoting recovery from chronic illness.
- Fostering positive emotions and increasing our confidence.
- Establishing a general sense of peace of mind, contentment, and positive direction in our life.

When considering the benefits of healing meditation, it is important to emphasize that healing is fundamentally about revealing our essential nature. Practices, therapies, and herbs can help us because the seed of well-being is already within us. The greatest gift that healing meditation offers is to reconnect us with that inner seed of well-being, and then to strengthen that connection.

Regardless of our age, gender, culture, or any other worldly labels, healing meditation can reward us with tangible benefits. However, to access the deepest benefits of healing meditation we need to realize that our happiness and well-being are our responsibility. How we feel is up to us, not to anybody else—not to our spouse, not to our colleagues, not to our doctor, not the weather, the economy, or the government. It is true that since we are all interconnected, these influences have an effect on our lives. Yet, in the intimacy of our being, we can choose how we want to feel despite external conditions.

Quoting meditation master Garchen Rinpoche: "When the mind is disturbed, one finds suffering anywhere, even in positive circumstances. If the mind is at ease and filled with love, one finds happiness even while surrounded by seemingly difficult outer circumstances." Through healing meditation, whether engaged in practice or as we go about our daily activities, as we develop a state of relaxed wakefulness, our heart grows more loving and kind. Then our body, energy, and emotions naturally heal. Such is the powerful gift of healing meditation.

Where Do the Healing Now Practices Originate?

The practices presented in *Healing Now* come from the ancient traditions of eastern medicine and from the people who practiced the Tao—the integral way of life—as an approach for living long, healthy lives and for spiritual development. For these ancient practitioners, well-being was the result of a lifestyle based on the observation of nature and its rhythms. Their lifestyle promoted efficient energy flow and harmony with their environment.

Through observation and insight, healing meditation practitioners understood that they could more easily sustain their physical health and inner balance by following the cycles and transformations of universal energies. Their deep understanding of life and the cosmos developed into a holistic medicine that included acupuncture, herbology, nutrition, therapeutic massage, breathing exercises, restorative movement, and meditation. Even though we live on the same planet as those ancient practitioners, our circumstances today are very unlike theirs. So, although rooted in their ancient wisdom, *Healing Now* presents a simple yet profound approach to healing meditation for our current times.

How To Practice

Healing Now is a practical book. Its purpose is to introduce you to the practice of healing meditation in a direct and simple way so that you can immediately begin to develop your own practice. In fact, you can begin your first practice right now: Just read the following four steps, then set the book down and continue to observe your breathing for three minutes.

1. Wherever you are, without attempting to change anything, bring your attention to your breathing.
2. Be aware of your breathing as the air comes in.
3. Be aware of your breathing as the air goes out.
4. Allow your body and mind to relax as you observe the natural rhythm of your breathing.

Congratulations. You have completed your first healing meditation practice. Easy and enjoyable, right? This seed practice is the foundation of all the other practices you will learn in *Healing Now*. You can go back to this simple practice any time to feel well, calm, and clear. Now, while savoring your first healing meditation practice, let's discuss how to get the full benefit from this book.

Healing Now presents four categories of meditation practices: Healing with the Breath, Healing with the Smile, Healing with Sound and Color, and Healing with Self-Massage. Each of these categories corresponds to a chapter. Within each chapter, each practice presents an introduction to the practice, instructions on how to practice, some of the most important healing benefits of that practice, and then some further practice insights to help you deepen your understanding. Even though each practice is different, all of them share the same goal: to help you experience well-being by promoting energy flow, reinforcing positive feelings, and cultivating a loving, wakeful mind that embraces everything and everyone.

It is best to follow the practices in the order in which they are presented. Each practice is complete in itself. At the same time, as you follow them in order, you will see that each practice gives you the foundation for the next practice and enriches your understanding of the practice you have just completed.

You are encouraged to spend two weeks in each of the practices of chapters 1, 2, and 3. Dedicating two full weeks to each of the practices in each of these chapters will allow you to become familiar with the techniques and to experience their cumulative benefits. Once you have completed all the practices in the book, you can choose whatever practices you feel more drawn to and make your own practice structure.

While all the practices that *Healing Now* presents offer profound healing benefits, the self-massage sequence from chapter 4 provides especially swift results and makes all the other practices more effective. For this reason, you should incorporate the self-massage right from the beginning. At the end of your healing meditation session, or by itself before bed, practice the self-massage to spread joyful healing energy throughout your whole body. Once you are familiar with the self-massage sequence, it takes only 3–5 minutes to complete.

Ideally, set aside thirty minutes to an hour daily to study and practice healing meditation. If possible, divide your practice time between morning and evening, around the same time every day. Healing meditation practice is especially beneficial after waking up and before going to bed. Practicing during these times allows your healing meditation to frame your day: in the morning it prepares you for your activities in the world, centering your mind, awakening your creativity, and experiencing love and joy in your heart; at night it prepares you to rest well, restoring your physical body, and allowing your mind and spirit to become more aware within the dream and deep sleep states.

It is beneficial to always practice in the same place. Having a dedicated space for your healing meditation encourages you to practice regularly and also makes your practice more enjoyable. It can be a whole room, a walk-in closet, or simply a corner of an apartment. You can create a simple shrine with a candle, a bowl of water, flowers, and an image of a teacher who inspires you to heal and to be a better person. However, make sure not to wait until you have the "perfect" place to start practicing. You can simply start your practice sitting on your bed or in your living room chair. What is most important is to practice.

The best way to practice is sitting cross-legged or on a chair that allows your spine to be straight but relaxed. Lying-down practice might be easier if your overall health is compromised and you don't feel well. Also, lying-down practice can be useful when it precedes a restorative nap or to help you fall asleep at night.

In addition to your regular daily practice, most of the practices in *Healing Now* are simple enough that you can make use of them any time of the day and anywhere you are. Standing in line at the store, sitting at the office, or lying down while reading a book to your kids at bedtime, for example, are moments where you can incorporate the techniques you will learn in this book.

Reflecting On Our Motivation

Understanding our motivation for practicing deserves special attention. There are two types of motivation: the first is personal, the second is altruistic.

In general, the reason why we begin to practice healing meditation is to improve our personal circumstances. We might want to improve our health, balance our emotions, calm our mind, maintain our well-being, develop our creativity, or find our path in life, to name a few examples. Our personal motivation is crucial because it is what brings us to the practice and sustains our enthusiasm to continue to practice. Yet, as crucial as it is, it is limited to our self-centered sense of "I, me, mine."

The second type of motivation—the altruistic motivation—expands beyond the focus on "just me." In what for many of us is an immense leap beyond selfishness and attachment, our altruistic motivation brings us to genuinely consider that the happiness and well-being of all other sentient beings, both friends and foes, is as important as ours.

Like the ocean and the countless waves born from it, the essence of all beings is one, yet that essence manifests in innumerable ways. For this reason, because everyone and everything that exists shares the same essence, our personal practice has the boundless potential to benefit all beings. When, at the beginning of our practice session, we give rise to this altruistic motivation—wishing that all beings, without exception, experience joy, well-being, and awakening—the benefit of our practice extends from our limited sense of I-ness to become as vast as the whole infinite existence.

Both motivations are precious, but the altruistic motivation is especially valuable. By expanding our field of intention, the virtues of our heart can mature from the limited "me" to the universal "we." In this way, we can heal from the illusion of separateness from others that is at the root of many health conditions and regain the experience of our shared divine nature.

Setting Up Our Motivation

For your personal motivation, think of what you would like to accomplish in your life through your practice: Do you want to heal from an illness? Do you want to improve your personal relationships? Do you want to feel more relaxed and at ease? Write or think what you want to accomplish and experience. An example could be:

> I am going to practice healing meditation to feel calmer when things get overwhelming at work, to have more patience with my family, and to improve my digestion.

After you read or think your personal motivation, let it rest in your mind for a minute, connecting with the feeling of having accomplished it.

Now, to state your altruistic motivation, you can use the following words:

> I am going to practice healing meditation to benefit both myself and all other sentient beings without exception. May my practice generate an infinite ripple of healing, well-being, and awakening across all time and space. May the illnesses of all beings be healed and may they never occur again. May my practice bring joy and clarity to all beings, helping all of us become aware of our perfect essence. May we have the courage to recognize the same perfect essence within everyone and everything. May this recognition awaken healing, joy, peace, and love within each of us throughout all existence.

After you read or think your altruistic motivation, let it rest in your mind for a minute, awakening inside your heart a feeling of joyful love towards all beings.

As you continue to practice your personal and altruistic motivations, the benefits will extend throughout the rest of your day, making you more aware of how to accomplish your personal goals and how to be more in harmony with your environment.

Dedicating the Benefit Of Our Practice

As we begin our practice session with our personal and altruistic motivations and then practice healing meditation techniques, we conclude our practice session dedicating the benefit of our experience to all beings without exception.

Even though our motivation and our dedication might seem similar, they are different: our motivation expresses the intent of what we are about to do; our dedication offers the results of what we have accomplished.

Completing our session with the dedication is like depositing the results of our practice into our spiritual savings account. It is by increasing the funds in that spiritual savings account that our personal well-being becomes more stable and our wisdom and realization unfold.

Like sharing a wonderful meal we have just cooked, we dedicate the benefit of our practice to share the joy, well-being, and wholeness we have awakened within us during our healing meditation session. Because in essence the minds of all beings are one, from our mind we can radiate the results of our practice across the infinite vastness of being to awaken joy, love, and kindness into the heart of all.

One way to dedicate your practice is to read the following words:

> By the merit of having practiced healing meditation for the benefit of myself and all other beings, may all beings, without exception, be well and happy, may there be peace in all lands, prosperity in all households, and joy in all hearts, across all time and space. And may all the motivation prayers made for the well-being of beings become a reality.

Then, after you have read the dedication, feel the joy of knowing that all beings—especially those you know who are in most need and those with whom you have any pending situation to resolve—benefit from the finest healing energies awakened through your practice.

Practice Diary

While it is not required, it can be very useful to keep a practice diary. Writing things down offers a powerful support for your healing meditation journey because it helps track the progression of your practice. Besides supporting you in the short term, keeping a practice diary also benefits you in the long term. When weeks, months, or years later you go back to your diary, you will remember details that most likely you had forgotten.

You can write in your practice diary any time of the day. Usually, it is helpful to write some notes after your daily sessions, since your practice is still fresh in your mind. Two other ideal times to write are after waking up, when you can write down about how you slept and note any interesting dreams; and before bed, where you can reflect on how your practice helped you during your day.

At the beginning of your diary, you can write down your initial personal motivations that lead you to practice healing meditation in first place. You can read these at the beginning of each practice session to set your personal motivation for practice. As you continue practicing, you can also write down modifications and additions to your personal motivation for practice as they happen.

The same applies for the dedication of your practice. If, instead of using the suggested motivation statement from above, you prefer to make your own, you can use your journal to write down your personal dedication.

Example of a Healing Meditation Session

It is best to practice healing meditation following a consistent structure. The following practice session suggestion includes all the aspects presented above:

1. Begin by expressing and reflecting on your personal and altruistic motivations.
   a. Express your personal motivation for practicing and reflect on it.
   b. Read the suggested altruistic motivation statement or express it in your own words and reflect on it.
2. Continue with the healing meditation you are working on.
   a. Read the details of the practice you are working on.
   b. Set a timer for the number of minutes you want to practice your healing meditation.
   c. Practice your healing meditation.
   d. Follow with the Dry Bath self-massage (chapter 4).
3. Finish by dedicating your practice for the benefit of all beings.
   a. Read the suggested dedication statement or express the dedication in your own words.
   b. Feel the joy of knowing that your practice benefits all beings.

After completing your healing meditation session, continue with your daily activities feeling revitalized, centered, and clear. Whatever you do and wherever you go, sustain a gentle sense of wakeful well-being. Allow your practice to help you become kinder and more loving with others and yourself. When you practice before bedtime—or before a nap—let the soft awareness of well-being ferry you into the blissful cycle of restorative sleeping and insightful dreaming.

As you read *Healing Now* and practice its teachings, keep in mind that healing is more about *being* than *doing* and more about *feeling* than *thinking*. Therefore, make sure to have fun and enjoy yourself, which is already a big part of the healing process and path to well-being.

May you, and all who come in contact with you, benefit vastly from your practice of the teachings in *Healing Now*.

Note: A guided audio and video meditation program accompanies this book. To access these meditations, go to:

www.joyfulheartinstitute.com/healing-now

I

HEALING WITH THE BREATH

"The Lord formed man of the dust of the ground,
And breathed into his nostrils and his face
The breath and Spirit of life;
And man became a living soul."
~Genesis 2.7

in and out, letting your mind rest on the flow of the breath of life.

For beginners, the suggested starting practice time is three minutes. After you have completed three minutes, you can stand up and stretch or walk a few steps and then sit again to observe your breathing for another three minutes. You can repeat observing the breath for three minutes followed by a short break as many times as you want.

Although three minutes might seem a short practice time, as soon as you start practicing you might realize that observing your breathing is challenging because your attention tends to quickly slip back into your habitual, continuous stream of thoughts. As a remedy to the natural tendency to distraction, observing your breath helps you train in being open and relaxed while sustaining firmness and focus.

During your practice, when you realize your attention has wandered away from your breathing, rejoice that you found yourself and regained awareness. Then, with tenderness, bring your attention back to the breathing cycle, as you would help a little child who has wandered off her bed sleepwalking. By conditioning your mind in this way, gradually you will be able to apply the same approach of reestablishing and sustaining loving, mindful awareness during all your daily activities.

As you become more comfortable with the practice, you can extend the practice time. However, when deciding the length of your practice, it is better to practice for a short time so that your mind stays aware and fresh rather than attempting a long practice where your mind keeps wandering or you fall asleep.

Awareness of breathing—breathing the life of life—is the treasure of the wise. Take advantage of it anytime, anywhere.

BREATHING 101

Breathing is our life's most basic rhythm. Even though commonly we are barely aware of it, breathing keeps us alive and influences every aspect of our being, including conscious and unconscious aspects. All our activities and experiences—physical, energetic, emotional, mental, and spiritual—are intimately related to how we breathe. Knowing the basics of how our breathing works can motivate us to maximize its healing and rejuvenating power.

On average, an adult breathes 15 times per minute: We breathe about 21,600 times per day; 650,000 per month; and about 8 million times per year. If we live to be one hundred, this amounts to 800 million breaths. Each of these single breaths is the direct experience of the life of our life, here and now.

Breathing is the result of the respiratory and circulatory systems working together: To keep us alive, our respiratory system (Fig. 1.1) brings in air, and our circulatory system spreads the contents of this air across our whole body. If either the respiratory or the circulatory system fails, cells start to starve due to the lack of oxygen and the accumulation of waste materials. We can live without food or water for days but being oxygen-deprived even for as few as three minutes can permanently damage the brain and cause death.

When we breathe in, we take air into our lungs through our nose or mouth: Even though the air we breathe in is invisible and appears empty, it is a mixture of gases, mainly nitrogen, oxygen, argon, carbon dioxide, and water vapor. Of all these components, the most important is oxygen, which is the essential element to energize and sustain our life.

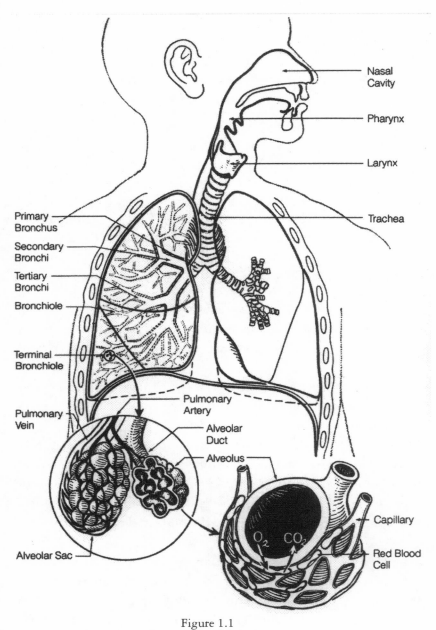

Figure 1.1
The respiratory system.
(Image Source: NCI - AV-0000-4101)

While in the womb, a baby's lungs are filled with amniotic fluid: During the gestation period, a baby receives oxygen from her mother through the umbilical cord attached to the placenta, the sac inside where the baby grows. The placenta is filled with amniotic fluid, a liquid made mostly of water, nutrients, and antibodies to support the baby's immunity. Amniotic fluid fills the lungs and helps them develop. Toward the end of the pregnancy, the baby begins to practice breathing with periodic inhaling and exhaling of amniotic fluid. During the birth process, the baby releases the fluid from her lungs. Once the baby is born, her lungs take over the breathing process.

All our body parts are made of breathing cells: Our body is made of about 400 trillion individual working units called cells. Even though independent from each other, our cells work together performing approximately 40 trillion functions and chemical reactions every second so that we can live our life. Even simple, daily activities like preparing breakfast, walking to our office, or writing an email involve the cooperation of trillions of breathing cells that require oxygen as their main energy source. That oxygen comes in with our breathing.

Our body breathes out metabolic waste: As a car requires gas to run and produces exhaust while using that gas, our body requires oxygen as fuel, and as it uses that fuel, produces waste that needs to be removed from our system. Inside our lungs, the oxygen contained in air is absorbed into our blood stream and sent to the rest of our body for the process of cellular breathing. During cellular breathing, our cells give off carbon dioxide and water as waste products. When we breathe out, our body uses the exhaled air to remove those waste products, along with some fermentation toxins produced in our digestive system.

Exercise is essential to maximize our breathing power: Different activities and emotional states generate different breathing patterns based on the amount of energy they require. When we practice physical exercise, our muscles need to work more. This increased activity requires more oxygen to supply the increased cellular activity in our muscles. To fulfill this extra demand for oxygen, we need to breathe deeper and faster, toning our whole body and cleansing our respiratory system. Besides increasing the amount of oxygen available in our system, exercise is also essential to feel good because it makes our body release endorphins, chemicals that trigger positive feelings in our mind.

PRACTICE
"EXPLORING YOUR BREATHING"

How is your breathing? Have you ever taken time to explore what keeps you alive? Getting to know the qualities of our breathing can provide many benefits to the overall health of our body and mind. For this reason, in the second practice of this chapter we are going to explore how we breathe.

In *Exploring Your Breathing*, our main objective is to observe and reflect on the qualities of our breathing. In this exploration we'll be investigating our breathing without correcting or changing anything. We are not looking for right or wrong qualities. We simply acknowledge what is happening in our breathing. Then, we use this information to understand the relation between different breathing patterns and how we feel.

Exploring Your Breathing has four parts. Each part corresponds to one of the four qualities of breathing we are going to explore: breathing depth, breathing speed, breathing sound, and breathing rhythm-ratio. It is important to practice slowly. Take as much time as you need to explore each quality attentively. You can explore the four qualities in one single session or divide the whole exploration practice into several healing meditation sessions. If you decide to explore the four qualities in one single session, make sure to allow enough time to do each in a relaxed manner.

As you follow the directions, you will be asked to answer some questions. You can either write your answers in your practice diary, if you are writing one, or simply reflect about the answers mentally. Whichever way you prefer is fine; just make sure you spend time considering the questions and how they relate to your breathing.

1. *Breathing depth:* The first aspect of our exploration refers both to the amount of air exchanged during inhalation and exhalation as well as how deep the sensation of that exchange reaches in the body. To explore breathing depth:

1. Sit comfortably on a chair: Your spine straight but relaxed, the soles of your feet flat on the ground, your hands resting on your thighs, and the rest of your body at ease. (Fig. 1.2 and Fig. 1.3)
2. Take some time to feel, "I am in this place and in this body."
3. To help you stay focused, activate the intention, "I am going to explore the depth of my breathing."

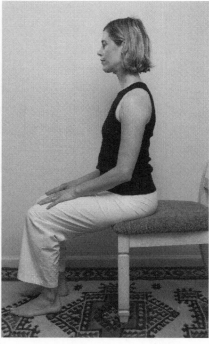

Figure 1.2
Sitting position front.

Figure 1.3
Sitting position side view.

4. To explore breathing depth as it relates to the amount of air exchanged, observe the flow of air coming in and out your body for as long as you need to answer the following questions:

   a. How much new air do you feel comes in?
   b. How much old air do you feel goes out?
   c. And, most important, does the amount of air going in and out feel sufficient or insufficient?

5. To explore breathing depth as it relates to physical reach, place your palms on top of your navel (Fig. 1.4) and observe the flow of air coming in and out your body for as long as you need to answer the following questions:

   a. Does your abdomen feel relaxed or tense?
   b. Can you feel your abdomen expanding and relaxing as air comes in and out?
   c. Is it a wide expansion and relaxation? Or is it barely noticeable?

6. Next, place your hands on the sides of your chest (Fig. 1.5) and observe the flow of air coming in and out of your body for as long as you need to answer the following questions:

   a. Can you feel your chest and ribcage expanding and relaxing as air comes in and out?
   b. Is it a wide expansion and relaxation? Or, is it barely noticeable?
   c. Does your breathing stay high in your chest? Or, is it evenly spread across your upper body?

7. After reflecting on those questions, bring your hands back to rest on your thighs and spend a few breaths observing the overall depth of your breathing. Then, answer the following questions:

a. Does your breathing ripple beyond your lungs towards your abdomen and your extremities? Or, does it feel mostly localized in the chest?

b. Does the depth of your breathing feel satisfying or not enough?

8. After you have considered these questions, relax for a few more breaths, letting go of any directions and simply enjoy being present and at ease.

2. *Breathing speed:* The second aspect of our exploration refers to the number of breaths we take per minute. To explore breathing speed:

1. Sit comfortably on a chair: Your spine straight but relaxed, the soles of your feet flat on the ground, your hands resting on your thighs, and the rest of your body at ease.

 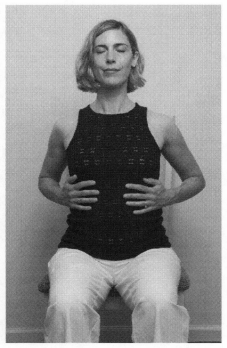

Figure 1.4
Observing abdominal movement.

Figure 1.5
Observing lateral movement.

2. Take some time to feel, "I am in this place and in this body."
3. Activate the intention, "I am going to explore the speed of my breathing."
4. To explore the respiratory rate of your breathing, first observe the speed at what air comes in and out of your body and answer the following question: Does it feel fast or slow?
5. Next, set a timer for one minute and count how many times do you breathe in one minute—one breath includes inhalation and exhalation.
6. Once you have counted your breaths per minute, relax for a few more breaths, letting go of any directions and simply enjoy being present and at ease.

3. *Breathing sound:* The third aspect of our exploration refers to the sounds produced as air goes in and out of our nose and mouth. These sounds can occur in the nose itself, in the throat, deeper in the bronchial tree, or in the actual lungs. To explore breathing sound:

1. Sit comfortably on a chair: Your spine straight but relaxed, the soles of your feet flat on the ground, your hands resting on your thighs, and the rest of your body at ease.
2. Take some time to feel, "I am in this place and in this body."
3. Activate the intention, "I am going to explore the sound of my breathing."
4. Then listen to the sound of air coming in and out of your body for as long as you need to answer the following questions:
   a. Can I hear myself breathing?
   b. Is my breathing loud or quiet?
   c. Is the sound of my breathing smooth or crackly?

5. After you have considered these questions, relax for a few more breaths, letting go of any directions and simply enjoy being present and at ease.

4. *Breathing rhythm-ratio:* The fourth aspect of our exploration refers to the pattern of inhalation and exhalation. Our breathing pattern has two main aspects: *breathing rhythm*, which refers to how speed, length, and timing are interrelated in our breathing; and *breathing ratio*, which refers to the length of the inhalation versus exhalation. To explore rhythm and ratio:

1. Sit comfortably on a chair: Your spine straight but relaxed, the soles of your feet flat on the ground, your hands resting on your thighs, and the rest of your body at ease.
2. Take some time to feel "I am in this place and in this body."
3. Activate the intention, "I am going to explore the rhythm and ratio of my breathing."
4. To explore the breathing rhythm, observe the flow of air coming in and out your body for as long as you need to answer the following questions:

   a. Does my breathing follow a regular or irregular pattern?
   b. Does my breathing feel even or choppy?

5. To explore the breathing ratio, as you observe the flow of air coming in and out your body, count the lengths of the inhalation and the exhalation. Start counting in your mind as you feel the air come in. Then, start another count as the air goes out. With that information, answer the following questions:

   a. Do my inhalation and exhalation have the same length or are they different?

b. If the lengths are different, which one is longer and which one shorter?

c. Do their lengths feel satisfactory or unsatisfactory?

6. After you have considered these questions, relax for a few more breaths, letting go of any directions and simply enjoy being present and at ease.

- Relaxing our body and mind.
- Developing focus and mental clarity.
- Becoming familiar with the qualities of our breathing.
- Realizing that how we breathe affects how we feel.
- Giving us confidence in our ability to support our health and healing.

PRACTICE INSIGHTS

Exploring Your Breathing offers us clear insight about how we breathe. Besides providing real-time information on how we breathe, exploring our breathing creates an awareness of our breathing qualities that carries to our daily activities.

Observing how our abdomen and rib cage move as we breathe is the easiest way to determine the depth of our breathing. If, as we inhale, our abdomen and our rib cage expand to the sides, front, and back, it means that we use a deeper range of breathing than if we are just moving only the middle part of our chest.

Shallow breathing limits the amount of oxygen our cells receive and challenges the metabolism of our body. The shortage of oxygen leads to internal disharmony, mental and emotional fogginess, energetic imbalance, and disease in general. Breathing superficially can be due to many factors, mostly lack of awareness and training, along with emotional and mental tension, stress, poor posture, tight clothing, heavy diet, and a sedentary lifestyle.

The speed of our breathing is an excellent indicator of our emotional and mental state. Faster, superficial breathing often happens when we are nervous, worried, or stressed since the heart tends to speed up to match our sense of emergency. In contrast, deeper breathing is calming. During states of deep relaxation, breathing slows down to the point that it feels as if it has stopped altogether for minutes. This impression of pausing our breathing happens because during deep relaxation our coarse nasal breath refines into a subtle whole-body breath through our skin, energy channels, and the crown of our head.

According to medical standards, the normal respiration rate for an adult at rest is 12 to 20 breaths per minute. During the day you can explore how different speeds feel to you and what causes you to breathe at different rates. Slower and deeper breathing enriches the quality of our daily experience and adds more life to our lives. Some spiritual traditions state that every being is born with an amount of breaths that determines their lifespan. Therefore, the slower our breathing, the longer our life can be.

Breathing sounds provide information about our overall health, the state of our mucous membranes, nose structure, emotions, and even about our diet. In general, the sound of our breathing should be smooth, almost silent. Sometimes we hear a rattling or phlegmy sound because we are congested. Other times, we may hear a small explosion as we exhale. This forceful sound reveals that we are unconsciously holding our breath until the body expels a sudden burst of air to release inner tension.

Ideally, we look for a breathing rhythm that is regular, with a similar length of inhalation and exhalation. This shows that the nervous system and the respiratory system are working in balance. While some lung and heart related medical conditions can cause irregular breathing patterns, in most cases irregularity is due to tension, stress, and anxiety.

To summarize, even though different situations will trigger and require different breathing qualities, in general, we attempt to establish a breathing that is deep, slow, silent and regular.

PRACTICE
"JOURNEY INTO DEEPER BREATHING"

"In this very breath that we now take
Lies the secret that all great teachers try to tell us."
~ Peter Matthiessen

Until now, the focus of our healing meditation journey has been on acknowledging, observing, and exploring the breath of life. Here, in *Journey Into Deeper Breathing* we start to consciously change the qualities of our breathing.

To deepen our breathing and maximize its healing potential, we divide the geography of our respiratory system into three sections (Fig. 1.6): first, our abdomen and diaphragm; second, our lower and mid ribcage; and third, our shoulders and upper part of the ribcage. Even though these three sections work always together as one unit, to see how each one has a different effect on the breathing process we will focus on one at a time.

In *Journey Into Deeper Breathing* we become familiar with the inner geography of our breathing and expand its territory. This journey allows us to recognize that our breathing potential is much larger than what we use on a daily basis. Because breathing is the foundation of our life, growth, and enjoyment, this is a profound realization: not only is most of our breathing capacity untapped, our larger capacity as human beings is also untapped.

It is better to practice *Journey into Deeper Breathing* sitting on a chair with our spine straight but relaxed, the soles of our feet flat on the ground, our hands resting on the thighs, and the rest of our body at ease.

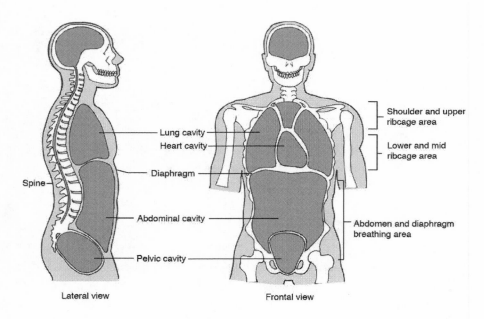

Figure 1.6
Bodily cavities and areas of breathing.

Abdomen and diaphragm:

1. Bring your attention to the flow of your breathing as you breathe naturally.
2. As you continue breathing, bring your attention to your lower abdomen and navel area. Observe if and how your abdomen moves as you inhale and exhale. Spend a few breaths doing this.
3. Smile to your abdomen and inner hips, sending happy feelings to the area. Invite all tensions—conscious and unconscious—to soften. Observe if and how your breathing changes. Spend a few breaths doing this.
4. Next, place your palms on your navel to feel the physical movement.
5. As you allow the area to soften with your smile, let

your breath gradually deepen into the abdomen. At the end of your exhalation, gently squeeze your abdominal muscles to release some extra air. (Fig. 1.7) As you inhale, observe and feel the abdomen expanding and relaxing with a wider range. Don't force or exaggerate your breathing. Combine a gentle extra pressure with your natural breath as your loving smile softens your abdomen, waist, and hips.

6. Spend three more minutes breathing in this way.
7. Then rest, breathing naturally. Can you feel how much the range of expansion and contraction widens after exhaling in this way?

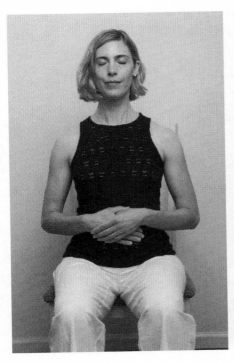

Figure 1.7
Guiding exhalation in the abdomen.

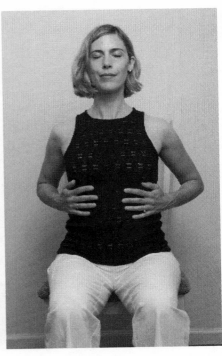

Figure 1.8
Guiding exhalation in the middle area.

Lower and middle ribcage:

1. Bring your attention to the flow of your breathing as you breathe naturally.

2. As you continue breathing, bring your attention to the lower and middle ribcage, on the front, sides, and back. Observe if and how the ribcage expands and relaxes as you inhale and exhale.

3. Smile to your ribcage, chest, and back, sending happy feelings all around the area. Invite all tensions—conscious and unconscious—to soften. Observe if and how your breathing changes. Feel if there is more expansion to the sides, front, and back as you inhale and exhale. Spend a few breaths doing this.

4. Next, place your palms on the sides of your chest, in a comfortable position.

5. As you exhale, use the muscles of your ribcage to gently squeeze out as much air as you can—be firm but without being forceful or creating tension. (Fig. 1.8) Once it feels you are completely out of air, softly try to squeeze a little bit more. (Important: Do this only while sitting or lying down. It is possible that it will make you feel lightheaded).

6. As a response to having exhaled so much air out, the body will need to take a large inhalation. Let it do that naturally without interfering. Once it reaches the peak of the inhalation, again apply light but constant force to let go of as much air as you can. See if now you can exhale even a bit more.

7. Repeat the deeper exhalation and inhalation three times.

8. Then rest, breathing naturally. Can you feel how much the range of expansion and contraction widens after exhaling in this way?

Shoulders and upper ribcage:

1. Bring your attention to the flow of your breathing as you breathe naturally.

2. As you continue breathing, bring your attention to your shoulders and upper ribcage. Observe if and how your shoulders and upper ribcage expand and relax as you inhale and exhale.

3. Smile to your shoulders, upper back, neck, and face, sending happy feelings all around the area. Invite all tensions—conscious and unconscious—to soften. Observe if and how your breathing changes. Feel if your upper ribcage and shoulders expand more upwards, front and back, as you inhale. Spend a few breaths doing this.

4. Next, place your hands on your shoulders. (Fig. 1.9) If that is uncomfortable for your neck, you can raise your elbows as you inhale and lower them as you exhale.

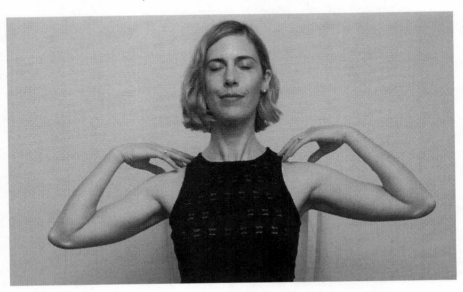

Figure 1.9
Exploring the upper range of breathing.

41

5. Without being forceful, use your upper ribcage muscles to apply a gentle effort as you exhale. Feel how the range of expansion and contraction widens in the upper part of the lungs.
6. Repeat the deeper exhalation and inhalation three times.
7. Then rest your arms and continue breathing naturally. Can you feel how much the range of expansion and contraction widens after oxygenating the upper lungs in this way?

Uniting the three sections:

1. As you inhale, follow this sequence: Abdomen relaxing and expanding; chest and back expanding to the sides and the front; shoulders and upper back expanding upwards and to the sides. Remember to let this happen lightly.
2. As you exhale, follow the reverse sequence: Applying light pressure with the shoulders and upper back downward and towards the inside; applying light pressure with the chest and back; softly contracting the abdomen. Remember to let this happen lightly.
3. Repeat steps 1 and 2 for three complete rounds. Then rest, breathing naturally, enjoying the experience of deep oxygenation. As you get used to the practice, you can increase the number of repetitions to 27.

HEALING BENEFITS

- Increasing the depth of our breathing to benefit our whole body.
- Rejuvenating our body and mind by helping all our cells to absorb more oxygen, releasing toxins and tension.

- Improving our respiratory and immune functions by deeply oxygenating our lungs.
- Toning our digestive and elimination system by relaxing our diaphragm and abdominal muscles.
- Learning to use our breathing to develop energetic integrity.

PRACTICE INSIGHTS

The key to practicing deeper breathing lies in extending the exhalation. The more air we let out, the more our body will naturally want to take back in. For this reason, we make the exhalation the emphasis of the breathing cycle.

At the beginning, we empty ourselves. As we exhale, we let go of stress, worries, tensions, blockages, and illnesses. We let go of anything that is not helping us thrive. With the inhalation that follows, we let ourselves be flooded with healing, joyful, loving energy, and we invite the renewed air exchange to transform into whatever we require at the moment to develop and sustain our well-being.

In the first part of the practice, your abdomen might expand and relax in different ways. Sometimes it will expand as you inhale, sometimes it will expand as you exhale. Explore to find what feels better. There is no rush. Take your time. In the second and third parts of the practice, we use areas of the lungs, especially the upper lungs, which are rarely exercised. Experience what happens to your body and your mind as you air and renew them. *Journey Into Deeper Breathing* provides you with an upgraded experience of your breathing possibilities. Enjoy the discovery.

POSTURE, HEALING, AND BREATHING

Our posture has a direct effect on how we breathe and how we feel: An optimally aligned posture allows us to breathe deeper and helps us feel better; a poorly aligned posture limits the capacity of our lungs and makes us feel tired and stressed.

Simple, right? Yet, even though the difference between properly and poorly aligned postures seems common sense, we often sit and stand as if we were contortionists, slouching forward or hunching our back, pushing the rib cage against the lungs and other inner organs and glands.

Besides limiting the depth of our breathing and decreasing the optimal functioning of our body, poor posture directly contributes to tension and pain in the neck, shoulders, and low back, causing body discomfort. Poor posture also contributes to pain indirectly because it puts pressure on the nervous system, triggering stress.

Don't despair, though. The solution is simple. Improving our posture is a quick fix that can be easily implemented throughout the day. By standing and sitting up straight, our ribcage expands, opening space for our lungs, heart, and digestive organs. Once our lungs, diaphragm, and abdomen are free from postural restrictions, more air can enter and leave our body with ease, helping us produce energy and eliminate waste more efficiently.

Improving our posture can also help us alleviate chronic neck, shoulder, and back pain. As we straighten our spine and relax our shoulders, our body returns to a healing posture that reduces inflammation and promotes relaxation and well-being.

We just need to find a way to remember to sit and stand straight and relaxed. Programming an alarm in our phone or computer to reminds us to check our posture every hour, for example, will work wonders.

Deeper, conscious breathing and regular physical activity will also provide immediate results to improve our posture and balance body mechanics. Just as our posture affects how we breathe, the way we breathe affects our posture. As our lungs and belly expand and relax following the breathing pattern, our spine straightens, massaging our internal organs and nervous system in a ripple effect that reduces stress, regulates heart function, lowers blood pressure, and facilitates digestion.

On the next page, there are suggestions for improving posture when sitting, standing, or lying down. You don't need to practice these suggestions on their own for two weeks each, as with the other practices in this book. Instead, use whatever of these posture suggestions is appropriate when practicing healing meditation as well as for the rest of your daily activities.

Once you start correcting your posture, your body might feel uncomfortable. This is normal, since your body is used to certain postures. But if you keep reminding yourself to correct your posture with gentleness, your body will get used to the new posture as the new normal.

DIRECTIONS

If sitting on a chair: Sit toward the edge of the chair, keeping your back straight but relaxed. Feet are flat on the ground, connecting your body with the Earth. Ankles and knees are in a vertical line. Knees and hips are in a horizontal line. Palms and hands rest on the thighs. Align the center abdomen, the center of the chest, and the center of the head. Tuck the chin slightly in. Make your tongue lightly touch your upper palate. Keep your gaze soft, looking forward past the tip of your nose or straight. Feel as if someone is pulling you up by your hair to help you lift the crown of your head, connecting your mind and spirit with Heaven. (Fig. 1.10 and Fig. 1.11)

If standing: Stand straight and tall. Place your feet about shoulder-width apart. Distribute your weight between the points on the sides of the ball of your feet and the heel. (Fig. 1.13) Bend your knees slightly. Let your arms hang naturally down the sides of the body. Pull your shoulders backward. Raise your chest slightly up and out. Level your head in line with your shoulders, not forward or backward. Follow the rest of the steps as explained in *If sitting on a chair.*

If sitting on the ground: In a clean area, place a small mat to sit on. Use a pillow, a block, or a towel to elevate your hips and help you keep your back straight. Cross your legs in any position that feels comfortable. (Fig. 1.12) Follow the rest of the steps as explained in *If sitting on a chair.*

If lying down: Lie flat on a firm surface. Elevate your knees with or without the help of a pillow. (Fig. 1.14) Place the lowest support for your head that you feel comfortable with, using a thin pillow or even a couple of books with a towel on top. Rest the hands at your side or on your abdomen.

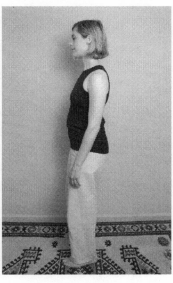

Figure 1.12
Sitting on the ground.

Figure 1.13
Standing (side view).

47

 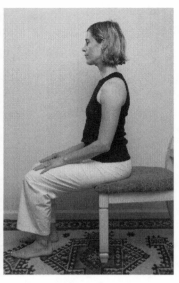

Figure 1.10
Sitting position frontal view.

Figure 1.11
Sitting position side view.

Figure 1.14
Lying down with raised knees.

PRACTICE
"THE THREE ALIGNMENTS: POSTURE, EMOTIONS, AWARENESS"

After learning about how our posture affects our breathing and well-being, we revisit the first practice, *Breathing the Life of Life*. Again, we become aware of our breathing, but now we do it with a properly aligned posture.

Even though in the previous section we only referred to physical posture, it is important to realize that there are three main levels of personal alignment: physical or outer, referring to the efficient positioning of our different body parts; emotional or internal, referring to our focus on positive emotions and actions based on the most noble virtues of the human heart; and mental or unseen, referring to how we sustain our attention in the here and now.

While these three levels of alignment depend on each other, it is easier to focus first on the physical level because our body is obvious and concrete. Having a proper physical posture helps us align our energetic channels, contributing to the healthy flow of blood and vital force throughout our body. When our energetic channels are flowing smoothly, our internal organs work better, we feel good, and our emotional view of life is upbeat and optimistic. An aligned physical posture also helps anchor the mind in the present moment, making us feel aware and awake.

DIRECTIONS

1. Following the posture guidelines from before, make your body comfortable, ideally sitting or lying down.
2. Become aware of your breathing.

3. Make any necessary adjustments to make sure your breathing feels free and satisfying.
4. Feeling at ease and breathing freely, feel a positive emotion such as love, joy, kindness, satisfaction, safety, or abundance. If you need to, bring to mind someone or something that makes you feel that way. Then, let go of the story and stay with the positive feeling.
5. Mix that positive emotion with your breathing as it comes in and out. As you breathe in, feel the breath carrying the good feelings inward, expanding through the whole body. As you breathe out, feel the breath expanding the good feelings outward, surrounding you.
6. Feeling at ease and breathing freely, experiencing the positive emotional state. Become aware of yourself, here and now, as the one who is experiencing breathing positive feelings with a good physical alignment.
7. Effortlessly, within the open vastness of your being, keep experiencing the alignment of those three qualities—proper posture, positive emotion, and self-awareness—breathing for at least three minutes.

HEALING BENEFITS

- Recognizing how our posture affects how we breathe and how we feel.
- Helping our inner organs work better by giving them more room to work.
- Experiencing how the body feels at ease.
- Creating connection between aligned posture and happy emotions.
- Finding inner support to align our actions with our desires.

We are the expression and extension of life itself. As such, our body, the guesthouse for our divine being, is an intelligent vibrational entity formed by trillions of self-regulating cells. Within our incredible body, well-being and illness manifest as the opposite expressions of the same energy and consciousness. How we align our posture, emotions, and awareness greatly influences where we find ourselves on the spectrum between well-being and illness: efficient alignment, joyful emotions, and open energetic flow promote well-being; physical misalignment, energetic stagnation, and repetitive, limiting patterns promote illness.

As long as we are at ease and aligned, energy naturally moves through our system, feeding, cleaning, and renewing us. In this way, we remain tuned to the universal natural rhythm of well-being. On the other hand, inefficient alignment blocks our natural well-being, leading to physical exhaustion, internal accumulation of toxins, and mental tension. If temporary misalignment persists, chronic illness develops.

By practicing *The Three Alignments* we learn to sustain an aligned posture, a joyful loving heart, and a wakeful mind. This blend of personal alignments facilitates conscious breathing, encourages positive emotions, and makes us present and aware. Aligned and well established in the now, we stop being like autumn leaves pushed here and there by the wind, at the mercy of circumstances. Instead, we become like the branches of a willow tree, flexible yet well anchored in the trunk, able to go through life's changes with softness but firmness.

The Three Alignments is an outstanding meditation practice that reminds us to embody loving, mindful being as the foundation of our healing and well-being, especially when our busy lives offer many opportunities to feel frustrated and tense. Through observing our breathing and sustaining purposeful physical, emotional, and mental alignments, we become more easy-going and flexible, while abiding firm and focused on our higher purpose.

BENEFITS OF DEEPER, CONSCIOUS BREATHING

While deeper, conscious breathing is not a substitute for medical help, it can be one of the best prevention tools you have to avoid needing medical help in the first place. By observing your breathing and making the necessary adjustments to optimize it, you can improve your quality of life and increase longevity, not only in well-being and length, but also in depth of experience of the moment.

The purpose of the practices presented in *Healing Now* is to help you enjoy the exceptional benefits that deeper, conscious breathing can offer. To summarize its many benefits, regular, deeper, conscious breathing:

Rejuvenates the body and increases energy and stamina: What looks more vital, a stagnant pool of rotten water filled with larvae and green, bubbly sludge floating around, or a fresh flowing, crystal clear mountain stream? Our body has the potential to be the same as either of those two waters. Through deep breathing we can maintain a more energetic, younger, and healthier body, like the fresh flowing, crystal clear mountain stream.

Reduces tension, stress, and anxiety: Tension and stress constrict breathing. Shallow breathing reduces distribution of oxygen, the essential fuel all our body parts use. Our brain, only about 2% of our body weight, accounts for about 20% of the oxygen consumed by the whole body. Deep breathing means abundant resources for our brain and nervous system. Why wait to feel tense, though? We can use conscious, soft, natural breathing as a regular practice to be at ease, tone our nervous system, and feel happy.

Improves sleep quality, stabilizes good mood, and promotes faster recovery from depression: When our brain and glands are more oxygenated by the regular practice of deeper breathing, they more efficiently produce the neurotransmitters and hormone levels we require to feel well. As a result, the mind has an easier time shutting off at night, our emotions stay on the positive side, our self-esteem improves, and many of the symptoms of depression—lack of mental focus, impaired memory, poor decision making, lack of motivation, obsession, pessimism, and irritability—lessen or disappear.

Improves digestion and elimination: How we breathe has a direct effect on how we digest, absorb, and eliminate. As the lungs, diaphragm, and other muscles involved in breathing expand and contract, they massage the liver, stomach, pancreas, and intestines. The increased bodily oxygenation and elimination of waste reduces inflammation and promotes better absorption and assimilation. The relaxation we experience through deeper breathing helps our large intestine to let go of waste, promoting regular bowel movements and relieving constipation.

Helps the body to detoxify efficiently: Imagine opening the windows of a stuffy room to get fresh air in and let stale air out. Our lungs are the windows of our body. Thanks to our lungs and respiratory system we refresh, balance, and purify at all levels—physical, emotional, and mental. Deeper, conscious breathing supports the function of all the organs, especially the liver, kidneys, and heart. Deeper, conscious breathing also helps us eliminate waste residues from our body tissues efficiently. Efficient toxin elimination makes all body systems and processes work better, keeping us healthy.

Helps to optimize body weight: When our breathing supports the nervous system and digestion, keeping our weight under control is easier since our metabolism naturally works better. Also, by feeling calmer, we make better food choices and don't need to overeat to soothe our emotions. When our body and brain are better oxygenated, we feel better and sticking to an exercise program is easier.

Increases immunity: Using a deeper range of breathing capacity keeps the respiratory system, including nasal passages and sinuses, cleaner. This promotes better immunity, reducing allergies, colds, and infections. While deeper conscious breathing by itself might not completely eliminate asthmatic and allergic conditions, research shows that regular breathing practice reduces the severity and recurrence of symptoms.

Helps with menstrual cramps and hormonal irregularities: By its influence on blood flow, elimination of toxins, and production of hormones, deep breathing positively assists women through the different parts of the menstrual cycle, including improved fertility and easier menopause.

Improves posture: Constricted, shallow breathing makes the chest collapse, putting extra burden on the spine and the low back. Poor posture constricts breathing and diminishes the function of all our internal organs. As an antidote, deep breathing engages the muscles of the abdomen, diaphragm, rib cage, and upper part of the chest. It also straightens the spine and softens the shoulders and jaws. Therefore, deep, conscious breathing gradually corrects poor posture and establishes good habits.

Improves overall blood circulation: As we deepen and enhance our breathing, our body relaxes, allowing blood vessels to soften, improving blood circulation to all cells in the body and lowering blood pressure. With our blood more oxygenated, our heart receives more nourishment and is better cleansed. Because of its direct effect on the nervous system, deep breathing also regulates heart rate and has a positive effect on blood pressure.

Reduces pain and inflammation: Deep breathing promotes better irrigation of nutrients and drainage of waste from all areas of our body, therefore reducing inflammation and pain. Research shows that deep breathing causes the brain to release endorphins and enkephalins—hormones associated with happy, positive feelings. All body cells have receptors for these hormones and receive the "stop pain, feel well" message. Deeper, conscious breathing increases parasympathetic nervous tone, which reduces anxiety and stress caused by pain. Since it reduces tension, deeper breathing helps us to remain calmer mentally and deal with each situation with greater ease and humor.

PRACTICE
"CENTERING AND PURIFYING BREATHING"

Our physical body is an inert structure that receives vital force and support from its energetic counterpart, our energy body. The spark that initiates and supports our energetic body is triggered in the sinoatrial node, a structure inside our heart that is responsible for making our heart pump blood to the rest of the body. Contained in the blood that is pumped, the same energy that empowers our heart spreads across all our bodily systems, extending beyond and around us.

According to natural and energetic medicine, our body organizes its energetic field using 72,000 channels that surround and pervade our physical body. Out of those thousands of channels, the three most important are the ones that run from the lower abdomen up the spine to connect with the nostrils and the brain.

The Centering and Purifying Breathing, also known as *Alternate Nostril Breathing*, is one of the most important healing meditation practices because it keeps our body and mind healthy by maintaining a smooth flow of energy along those three main channels.

DIRECTIONS

Preparation:

1. Sit comfortably with your back straight but relaxed, your hands resting on the thighs, and the rest of the body at ease.
2. Take three relaxed breaths.
3. Awaken within yourself a feeling of openness, well-being, and optimism.

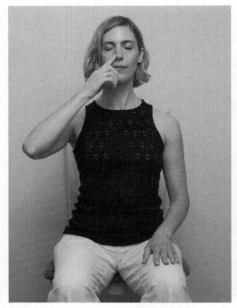 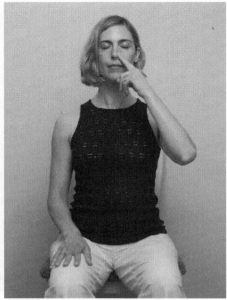

Figure 1.15
Inhaling through the left nostril.

Figure 1.16
Exhaling through the right nostril.

Clearing right channel:

1. With the index finger of your right hand, press the right nostril, blocking it. (Figure 1.15)
2. Inhale through the left nostril.
3. Hold your breath while you bring your right hand back to your lap. Still holding your breath, with the index finger of your left hand, block the left nostril. (Figure 1.16)
4. Exhale through the right nostril. Feel how any conscious or unconscious stress, tension, negative emotions, and illness leave the body and dissolve into space.
5. Lightly hold your breath while you switch hands: your left hand goes back to your lap; the index finger of your right hand blocks the right nostril to start the cycle again.

6. Repeat steps 1 to 5 a total of three times. With every breath, feel an increased sense of well-being, clarity, and joy.

Clearing left channel:

1. With the index finger of the left hand, press the left nostril, blocking it.
2. Inhale through the right nostril.
3. Hold the breath while your bring your left hand back to your lap. Still holding your breath, with the index finger of your right hand, block the right nostril.
4. Exhale through the left nostril. Feel how any conscious or unconscious stress, tension, negative emotions and illness leave the body and dissolve into space.
5. Lightly hold the breath while you switch hands: your right hand goes back to your lap; the index finger of your left hand blocks the left nostril to start the cycle again.
6. Repeat steps 1 to 5 a total of three times. With every breath, feel an increased sense of well-being, clarity, and joy.

Clearing central channel:

1. With both hands resting on your lap, breathe in slowly and deeply through both nostrils, feeling how the air goes down from your nose to the base of your abdomen or your feet.
2. Breathe out slowly, feeling how the air ascends from your lower abdomen or your feet, leaving your body out the crown of the head. Feel how any conscious or unconscious stress, tension, negative emotions, and illness leave the body and dissolve into space.
3. Repeat three times.
4. After completing the third round, feel healing,

golden light showering down from above your head, surrounding and filing your whole being.

Concluding:

1. Bask in the renewed warmth of positive qualities like love, joy, and well-being throughout your body and mind.
2. Breathe naturally for at least three minutes, resting in peace and openness, enjoying the experience of resting in the present moment.

- Cleansing the lungs, sinuses, and nasal passages.
- Purifying the energy channels and expelling stagnant energy from our system.
- Feeling present, focused, and grounded by integrating the physical body and the mind.
- Relieving symptoms of stress, anxiety, depression, and trauma, including headaches, tension, cravings, impatience, anger, and insomnia.
- Relieving exhaustion, regulating blood pressure, and supporting the cardiovascular system.

PRACTICE INSIGHTS

Our brain is divided into two equal parts called hemispheres. Each of these two hemispheres is responsible for coordinating different kinds of activities and relates to different emotions and personality traits. To maintain our well-being, it is important that the natural energetic flow between these two sides of our brain is smooth and keeps a regular rhythm.

To make sure the two sides of the brain and their corresponding activities stay balanced, our nervous system has an energetic rhythm that alternates its emphasis between the two hemispheres of our brain. This natural pulsation has its counterpart in our breathing, which alternates its emphasis from one nostril to the other one—the nasal cycle.

Due to causes such as sedentary lifestyle, fast and shallow breathing, poor diet, disconnection from nature, and overuse of technology, the natural pulsation of our brain loses its balanced rhythm. This unbalance causes one side of our brain to be overemphasized, affecting our overall health and the ways we feel about things.

Nowadays, one of the factors that most affects brain function is cell phone use. Due to the strong radiation cell phones emit, they overheat the side of the head where used most frequently. *Centering and Purifying Breathing* helps us refresh our brain and reduce damage from cell phone overuse.

Even though *Centering and Purifying Breathing* is an ancient healing meditation practice, it has been extensively researched in modern times for its many health benefits, especially related to the nervous system. Research shows that creating regularity in our breathing benefits our brain's energetic flow, providing regularity and stability in our physical body and mind, helping us experience emotions without dramatic ups and downs or obsessions.

The *Centering and Purifying Breathing* is one of the simplest healing meditations to remember and apply, yet one of the quickest to provide clear benefits. If you could only choose one exercise from this book to practice daily, it should be this one. Make it part of you daily routine just like brushing your teeth and showering.

PRACTICE
"BREATHING IN, MY MIND IS CALM;
BREATHING OUT, MY BODY IS RELAXED"

Most of us know that the quality of our thoughts and emotions directly affects our health and well-being. What most of us don't know is that we can choose what emotions to focus on and what to do with our thoughts.

Healing and well-being are in great measure about choosing what emotional path we want to follow. Because we don't know better, we often jump into the first emotion we feel and grasp it as revealing the truth and guiding our actions. For example, if we feel sadness, we say to ourselves, "I am sad, what can I do?" At first we might wrestle with the feeling of sadness. But this inner wrestling exhausts us. Then, exhausted, we accept sadness as the final truth and live with it.

It is true that things happen in our lives that challenge us. Faced by these challenges, emotions of anger, resentment, frustration, fear, worry, jealousy, and the like surface into our awareness. In essence, there is nothing wrong with these emotions. They are movements of energy within our human awareness. But, just because they surface doesn't mean we have to make them our reality.

Using a completely different approach, if with diligence we focus on the positive aspects of our life, regardless of how many apparent non-positives there might be, we release resistance and invite positive experience into our day-to-day lives. Instead of being defeated by circumstances, in the present moment—with our breathing as the carrier—we can align positive intention and sustained attention to infuse loving energy into all our cells and body systems.

When we deliberately focus on good feelings, positive thoughts, and uplifting emotions, the cells of our body have an easier time returning to natural balance. This healing renewal is possible because right now—and in every moment—our awareness commands our energy. Where we direct our energy affects our physical body. Therefore, we can bring healing to our body and mind by using clear intention and sustained attention.

This healing, optimistic vision is not an attempt to deny whatever challenges we might be facing. We are not naively painting a peachy view of an imperfect world. On the contrary, this practice is a deliberate and conscious choosing of how we want to feel and from where we want to find solutions. Against all worldly odds, we translate our will to be well and free into a crystal clear vibration that resonates through our whole being, as the note of a guitar resonates inside the guitar's body, around it and beyond.

By sustaining a positive view of our life and blending that view with our breathing—inviting the joyful energy to ride our breathing—we let go of tension and resistance, welcoming our body and mind back to well-being.

DIRECTIONS

1. Bring your attention to the flow of air coming in and out of your body.
2. Bring to mind a moment when you felt happy and relaxed. Focus on how the moment felt, not on the story of the moment.
3. Sustaining the positive feeling of that moment, as you inhale, think and feel: "Breathing in, my mind is calm." As you exhale, think and feel, "Breathing out, my body is relaxed."
4. Feel how the substance and sound of the breath vibrate with the words "calm" and "relaxed," and their meaning.
5. Keep blending the feeling "calm" with your inhalation

and the feeling "relaxed" with your exhalation for at
least three minutes.

6. Let go of the statements and rest in an open, clear, and
   joyful state of being.

- Promoting overall relaxation and calmness.
- Releasing physical tension and relieving pain.
- Training us to respond instead of reacting.
- Transforming unwanted emotional states into more
  desired and fulfilling emotional states.
- Cultivating patience and openness to life as it
  manifests, even if it's different than we expected.

PRACTICE INSIGHTS

Regardless of our current situation, in our life we all have
experienced calm and relaxing moments when we felt content, at
ease, and were enjoying ourselves. For some of us these moments
might easily come to mind. Some of us might need to dig deeper.
Yet, the memory of what joyful, calm, and relaxed feels like is
stored somewhere in our body and mind.

The feeling of calm and relaxed is like when, on a hot day,
someone hands us a fresh glass of our favorite drink. We take a big
sip and sigh, "Aaaaahhhh… Heaven." You know well how this
contentment and happiness feels. It's a mixture of relief, satisfaction,
joy, and pleasure. As you combine that feeling with your breathing,
your brain starts producing the happy neurochemicals that tell all
the cells of your body to go into well-being mode.

Using the full wording, "Breathing in, my mind is calm;
breathing out, my body is relaxed," provides a strong anchoring
for the practice. When you use the complete sentence, the inhaled
and exhaled breaths have similar length, which balances and
soothes the nervous system. Once you have become familiar with

the practice, you can switch to "I am calm" as you inhale, and "I am relaxed" as you exhale.

Any time of the day, if you experience a moment of strong dispersion or negativity, remembering the statement—"Breathing in, my mind is calm; breathing out, my body is relaxed"—will ground you in the reality that in the present moment all is well. Connecting positive mental states to your breathing gives you access to the blueprint of your divine being, which is joyful, abundant and resourceful.

You can change the combinations of words according to whatever personal dispositions you want to balance or whatever you desire at that moment. For example, if you tend to feel:

- Worried, you can use, "Breathing in, I feel safe; breathing out, I feel at peace."
- Lonely, you can use, "Breathing in, I appreciate myself; breathing out, I feel connected."
- Confused, you can use, "Breathing in, I am clear; breathing out, I know what to do."
- Shame, you can use, "Breathing in, I love myself; breathing out, I enjoy myself."

Whatever the wording you use, the key is to make sure you feel what the words mean. Blending the feeling with your breathing will inform the different layers of your being of your higher intentions. Use the essence of this practice in any form you want during the day to focus and sustain the feelings you are seeking.

PRACTICE
"RESTING IN THE NARROW GATES"

"Enter through the narrow gate."
~Matthew 7.13

"Come to me, all you who are weary and burdened.
I will give you rest."
~Matthew 11.28

Our breathing cycle has four parts: First, air comes in; second, there is a slight pause; third, the flow reverses and air goes out; fourth, there is another pause before air comes in again. In all the previous practices, we have focused on phases one and three, the moments when air comes in and goes out. Now we turn our attention to the resting moments, phases 2 and 4.

At first, the pauses in between the dynamic moments of incoming and outgoing breath seem subtle, as if almost ungraspable. But they are there, and it is that subtle, ungraspable quality that empowers them with great significance in our healing process. Becoming aware of—and maintaining uninterrupted awareness of—these empty spaces opens us to a whole new dimension of being and perceiving that can be expressed as returning to our source.

When our attention is able to rest on that which is empty, that without substance, a tremendous release of subtle yet powerful healing energy takes place. The energy of our awareness is released from the common objects of the senses—images, sensations, smells, flavors, sounds, and thoughts—that generate tension through constant attachment and refusal. Free from the constraints and worries of our daily world, the mind can rest in deep contentment.

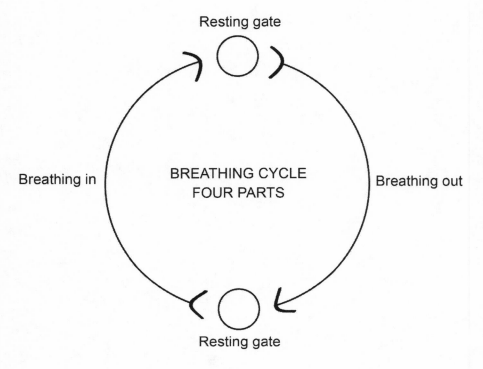

Figure 1.17
The four parts of our cycle of breathing.

According to the principles of healing meditation, these two openings, empty yet full, are precious moments where we can easily connect with the essence of our being. As our attention rests in these two openings, we experience the joy of remembering that what we call reality is only as real as last night's dream, or a rainbow—tangible yet unsubstantial, present but fleeting. As we recollect and experience, even if only glimpses, the boundless, essential nature of life, we soften and heal.

1. Bring your attention to the flow of air coming in and out of your body.
2. Become aware of the four parts of the breathing cycle: Air comes in, pause, air goes out, pause.
3. Observe these four parts for as many breaths as you need until you can recognize them clearly.
4. Switch the emphasis of your attention to the spaces—openings—in between breathing in and breathing out.
5. Feel the sensation that you experience in these two openings.
6. While the breathing cycle continues at a natural rhythm, softly rest your attention in the feeling of the openings for at least three minutes.

HEALING BENEFITS

- Learning to appreciate the nurturing beauty and spiritual significance of wakeful resting.
- Cultivating stability by connecting with the state of well-being that is always present within us.
- Recovering from the addiction to reenacting the past and to anticipating the future.
- Developing confidence in living an enjoyable and fulfilling life.
- Establishing a new personal foundation of being by switching from a constantly-busy attitude to a state of presence and ease.

PRACTICE INSIGHTS

Resting In the Narrow Gates blossoms from the previous healing meditation, *Breathing In My Mind Is Calm, Breathing Out My Body Is Relaxed.* When our mind is calm and our body relaxed, we can recognize our life as a double reality: a dynamic aspect—the part of us and the world around us that is constantly changing; and a witnessing aspect—the part of us and the world around us that is unchanging, ever present.

Recognizing this dual experience of reality heals by reminding us that while what happens in our life is important, it is not final. Life is action-packed and, at the same time, the essence of our being is simple and unaffected by external events, like the sky. Through this recognition we can engage in life in a more relaxed and playful manner because we are aware that even intense dramatic situations happen in the play of life, yet our fundamental nature remains unaltered. This understanding is a powerful antidote to relieve worry, fear, stress, and anxiety.

Our breathing perfectly mimics this dual reality: it is dynamic—air moves in and out; and it is static—there is always space in between the in and out movements. The pauses, or resting moments, represent the unchanging reality that holds the original blueprint of healing and well-being. The unchanging and witnessing aspect of our being is always present; it is our essential nature. Yet, to benefit from it, we need to become aware of it. As with a radio, we need to tune our dial to receive the broadcast we want to hear.

The healing power of *Resting In the Narrow Gates* comes from resting on that which is empty as the source and root of our solid being. Through experiencing rest, we learn that being and witnessing are deeply restorative. This renewed view releases a tremendous amount of energy that was previously invested in attempting to feel complete by making our life every time more and more complex. Instead, as we rest in the vast openness of our being, we discover simplicity as the foundation of a healthy and happy life. As we read in the *Tao Te Ching*, "Nothing is done, yet nothing remains undone."

Resting In the Narrow Gates is a gentle meditation practice. It requires no effort whatsoever. Simply guide your awareness to the sensation of openness that occurs in the spaces between the incoming and outgoing motions of air. Let your attention rest in the feeling of those spaces without forcefully holding the air in or out. As you practice, these pauses will become longer; yet, in reality, their length is irrelevant. What makes these pauses special is that they reveal the space where our outer—worldly and subject to illness—and inner—fully awakened and perfectly healthy—aspects of being are in balance.

PRACTICE
"THE BODY OF SPACE"

"What fills everything, inside, above, below and around,
Itself Being-Consciousness-Bliss,
Non-dual, infinite, without beginning or end, one only,
Know that to be who you are."
~Atma Bodha v. 56

In *The Body of Space* we oxygenate and renew our body parts by kindling cellular breathing. This practice guides us to one of the most insightful healing meditation experiences: realizing that we are not just this body. Our body is part of who we are, yes. But, in essence, the body is a guesthouse for our consciousness to embody and interact within the physical plane.

While, in theory, this may be easy to understand, most of us don't live in full understanding. Instead, because our body is what we are most used to, we constantly focus on it as our exclusive identity. Convinced we are this body, we dedicate an endless amount of energy to cultivate, sustain, and protect our body image. As the center of "I, me, mine," our identification and attachment to the body creates a strong separation from others.

This strong attachment leads to emotional and physical tension, causing or worsening imbalances in our inner organs and nervous system. As an antidote, The Body of Space directs us to recognize our body and the world as a vibrant space, not so solid but more flexible. As our experience of what we are widens, we open ourselves to a new life of endless possibilities. From the openness of vibrant space, connected to the source of healing and manifestation, our awareness can guide energy to manifest in the creative, physical world.

Preparation:

1. Sit or lie down comfortably, remembering the essential points of efficient posture.
2. Take three relaxing breaths. Let your body soften.
3. Bring your attention to the place and moment where you are. Let your mind be at ease.

Lower body:

1. Bring your attention to the left leg. Smile to it. Ascending from the toes, ankle, calf, shin, and thigh to left buttock area, imagine that the leg is empty inside.
2. As you inhale, feel that the air comes in from the tip of the toes, filling up the space inside the left leg, from the toes to the buttock area.
3. As you exhale, feel that the air goes out, releasing tension, pain, and anything uncomfortable. Repeat this cleansing of the left leg for three full breaths.
4. Bring your attention to your right leg. Ascending from the toes, ankle, calf, shin, and thigh to left buttock area, imagine that the leg is empty inside.
5. Smile to your right leg. As you inhale, feel that the air comes in from the tip of the toes, filling up the space inside the right leg, from the toes to the buttock area.
6. As you exhale, feel that the air goes out, releasing tension, pain, and anything uncomfortable. Repeat this cleansing of the right leg for three full breaths.
7. Feel both legs at the same time. They are breathing, empty yet vibrant. As you inhale and exhale, feel them spacious and rejuvenated.

Hips, genitals, abdomen, and chest:

8. Bring your attention to your genital area, hips, abdomen, and chest.

9. Ascending from the hips and genital area to the neck, feel that these areas are empty inside.

10. As you inhale, feel the vibrant energy of the breath filling up that empty space.

11. As you exhale, feel that the air goes out, releasing tension, pain, and anything uncomfortable. Repeat this cleansing breathing in the hips, genitals, abdomen, and chest for three full breaths.

12. As you inhale and exhale, feel the hips, genitals, abdomen, and chest at the same time. They are breathing, empty yet vibrant. As you inhale and exhale, feel them spacious and rejuvenated.

Arms, shoulders, and head:

13. Bring your attention to your left arm. Imagine it is empty inside. Smile to the arm and the open space inside.

14. As you inhale, feel that the air comes in from the tip of the fingers, to the left shoulder, filling up the space inside with soft but vibrant energy.

15. As you exhale, feel that the air goes out, releasing tension, pain, and anything uncomfortable. Repeat this cleansing for two more breaths.

16. Bring your attention to your right arm. Imagine it is empty inside. Smile to the arm and the open space inside.

17. As you inhale, feel that the air comes in from the tips of the fingers, to the right shoulder, filling up the space inside with soft but vibrant energy.

18. As you exhale, feel that the air goes out, releasing

tension, pain, and anything uncomfortable. Repeat this cleansing for two more breaths.

19. Feel both arms at the same time. They are breathing, empty yet vibrant. As you inhale and exhale, feel them spacious and rejuvenated.
20. Bring your attention to your head. Feel that it is relaxed and soft. We put very light emphasis on the head since we want to prevent any dizziness.

Whole body together:

21. Experience your whole body as one empty and spacious unit.
22. Feel the soft, vibrant energy of your breathing air come in and spread through that whole empty unit. Then let the air go out without any kind of effort, feeling at peace.
23. If there are any areas of tension, smile there and invite them to soften.
24. Do not exaggerate the breath or try to change it in any way. Simply breathe in; simply breathe out.
25. Gradually let the breath become a little slower and deeper than usual, at whatever pace feels comfortable.
26. As you keep breathing, let yourself start to experience an expansive feeling of love, well-being, and calmness.
27. Continue simply breathing in, simply breathing out, in this way for 5 to 20 minutes.
28. Then just rest in a state of openness.

HEALING BENEFITS

- Letting go of tension and regaining vitality.
- Learning how to sustain a wakeful state while deeply resting and restoring our body and mind.
- Developing energetic integrity and inner alignment.

- Helping us experience who we are beyond our physical form.
- Connecting with the underlying field of vital force shared by all beings.

Our body is a physical embodiment of the divine awareness and love that creates and supports the whole universe. Even though we might not be aware of it, this divine reality is held within every single one of our cells as our inner nature. This divine reality is also present within our mind as the basis of our thoughts, feelings, and self-awareness.

From modern science we learn that the world we perceive through our senses is not as real as it seems, nor is it the only reality there is. Modern science supports the ancient spiritual principles of healing meditation that tell us that, even though the world (which includes our physical body) is solid and tangible, at a deep fundamental level it is open space and as unsubstantial as a dream.

Practicing *The Body of Space* heals us by guiding us to experience subtler levels of our body beyond its dense physical form. From within the experience of those subtler levels, practicing *The Body of Space* initiates the dissolution of self-imposed limitations that occur based on the false conviction that we are only our physical body. Through deeply oxygenating our body parts, *The Body of Space* allows us to expand past fixed ideas such as "I am this body; I am what has happened to this body." As we begin to experience the vast openness of our being, tensions and limiting views soften because they don't have anywhere to adhere to.

The Body of Space also allows us to realize that our mind is not just our thoughts. Our mind has many layers, most of them unknown to our daily mental faculties. Sustaining the spacious calmness and vibrant experience of whole body breathing, we heal by unconsciously allowing different layers of our mind to dissolve old imprints that limit our inner and outer realities.

During your meditation session, keep in mind that *The Body of Space* is not a practice of doing, but a state of allowing and releasing. By releasing tension and allowing relaxation, well-being floods our being and our awareness awakens. Ideally, use *The Body of Space* lying down and preceding a recharging nap, as the introduction to conscious dreaming, and, of course, when falling sleep at night. It is perfectly fine to fall asleep as you practice.

OBSERVING HOW OTHERS BREATHE

After reflecting on the importance of breathing, observing how we breathe, and exploring different levels of breathing, we can expand our practice by observing how others around us breathe. Of course, we don't announce what we are doing—if we did we could come across as strange and make people uncomfortable.

Wherever we are, we can use our senses to observe how others breathe. As we discreetly observe them, we keep in mind that "observing others" doesn't mean "correcting others." Our practice is simply to observe how others breathe by looking, listening, and feeling, without being noticed and not making any comments.

Observing others breathe—including animals—is a profound practice. At first it might feel that we are just observing how they get air in and out. But if we observe with loving calmness, not judging them as doing it wrong or right, we might sense how their breathing habits relate to the state of their minds and their life situation at large. Even though most likely others will not notice our observation, for us it will establish an intimate connection with them, allowing us to connect with them and their essence beyond their life story and beyond how their life story activates our own life story. The close level of connection that observing others breathe creates will awaken a deeper respect, interest, and affection even towards strangers, regardless of how we perceive them outwardly.

Observing others breathe allows us to perceive in them the divine thread of life shared by all beings—the breath of life. Observing them participate in this seamless thread beyond description that enlivens all of us has the power to transform our relationships and how we experience the presence of others in our life. By observing the breath of life in others, we reconnect with the divine awareness that abides within each of us, the source of well-being, virtue, and mindfulness. Through our silent experience of their divine identity, we can be a mirror that reflects for others the exquisite joy of their being—one and the same with the exquisite joy of all beings.

THE SEAMLESS WAVE

"Seamless, unnamable,
it returns to the realm of nothing.
Form that includes all forms,
image without an image,
subtle, beyond all conception.

Approach it and there is no beginning;
follow it and there is no end.
You can't know it, but you can be it,
at ease in your own life.
Just realize where you come from:
this is the essence of wisdom."
~Tao Te Ching, 14

After considering and practicing different aspects of breathing, we now go back to the beginning. Like a wave returns to the ocean after reaching the shore, we return to simply breathing in and out. Now again we breathe at ease, letting go of any control, experiencing that universal, healing wave of life and awareness as our own being.

At first, when we are introduced to the magic of conscious breathing, we are told that our breath is a living pulsation shared by all beings, a seamless wave coming and going across the magnificent ocean of life. Although this description of our breath may initially sound too abstract and grandiose, it plants in us a seed of sublime bliss we feel compelled to grow by practicing the instructions we have received.

As we practice, our breathing grows slower and longer. This lengthening is not forced in any way. We don't try to slow down our breathing. We don't hold it. Lengthening of the breath—

longevity in depth of being—happens naturally as we reclaim our attention from distraction and bring it to rest on the in and out flow of air.

As our breath becomes slower, it also becomes deeper. Besides all the health-related benefits, this slower, deeper breathing is our scout into subtler aspects of being. Without a doubt, the seed of pure, divine awareness pervades all states of being. But as our breathing deepens and lengthens, our attachment to the physical body and world also softens. We then start developing insight beyond what our five worldly senses perceive.

With each slower and deeper breath, we become more grounded and less reactive to the constant stimulation that surrounds us. As our thoughts slow down, we begin to realize the futility of exhausting ourselves attempting to accomplish all the demands that are imposed on us by a world that in essence is a mirage.

As thought diminishes and becomes part of the landscape— instead of thought being the boss of us—we recognize a more expansive, inclusive, and spacious state of being. Beyond thought and beyond the habit of focusing outwards, we embark on an exquisite journey into the vastness of who we are. Slower, deeper breathing allows us to expand yet remain aware through increasingly steady presence. As the seed of divine plenitude within us has more space to shine, we soften and learn to be at ease with whatever life presents to us.

As it lengthens and deepens, our breathing enjoys itself as that seamless wave that vibrates across the vastness of all life. Even during the pauses, which also gradually lengthen, the dynamic pulsation of breathing ferries us from the ocean of being to the shore of becoming, and vice versa. As we read in the *Tao Te Ching*, breathing leads us to recognize the "ever present, seamless thread" that is our awareness, the field where all healing takes place.

Within the experience of the present moment, guided by our deeper, slower and relaxed breathing, anytime and anywhere, we discover a profound silence. At first, it seems like our breathing has become quiet. Over time, though, we realize this silence is not just the absence of nasal and throat sounds. This silence is the presence of a vibrant self-awareness that remains undisturbed by any external sound or attachment.

As when, after a storm, the agitated water of a lake calms down and we can see the bottom, in the presence of this vibrant self-awareness, thoughts dissolve, allowing us to experience the natural qualities of who we are. The soft, vibrant, silent sound of our breathing awakens us as the spontaneous symphony of life in the present moment.

In the timeless yet ever-changing here and now, our breathing becomes regular, balanced, and relaxed. It is regular because its rhythm is without fluctuations, without coming and going. As the life of our life, our breathing is regular since the wakefulness of self-awareness is no longer interrupted. It is balanced because it blends our sense of "I am" with the continuity of experience, regardless of external circumstances—nothing is external any longer, all life is an inner experience. Our breathing is relaxed because it doesn't catapult us into the future or the past. Instead it allows us, almost forces us, to remain in the here and now, aware and awake.

This is the true healing power of our breathing. Slow, deep, conscious, spontaneous, regular, balanced, relaxed. Breathe in, you are alive. Breathe out, let your joy shine.

II

HEALING WITH THE SMILE

"Sometimes your joy is the source of your smile,
But sometimes your smile can be the source of your joy."
~Thich Nhat Hanh

A QUEST FOR JOY AND SELF-LOVE

The *Healing Smile* is a simple yet deeply profound meditation practice. It is simple because we just smile to ourselves. It is profound because by smiling to ourselves, we love ourselves.

Loving ourselves is the foundation of our personal and collective healing. No matter how many vitamins and supplements we take, how many yoga and tai-chi classes we attend, how many hours we spend at the gym or how many relaxing vacations we go on, true healing will only happen once we are able to love ourselves where we need it most: in our heart and mind.

As an organized, systematic process to cultivate self-love, the *Healing Smile* has the power to awaken our natural ability to rejuvenate and to experience well-being. Pervasive like the warmth of sunlight, the *Healing Smile* infuses our physical, energetic, emotional, and mental bodies with a blissful awareness that helps us remember the joy of who we are and dissolve the gloom of who we are not.

Wherever we are in our lives and regardless of how we are feeling about ourselves, the *Healing Smile* empowers us to cultivate self-care and self-love by reminding us that loving attention, openness, and acceptance towards what or who we encounter in our journey through life needs to include the person closest to us: ourselves.

The *Healing Smile* invites us to awaken and sustain optimism by focusing on well-being. When we smile to our physical body with love and gratitude, we tune our skin, muscles, bones, inner organs, and glands to the frequency of our divine essence. From this state of inner connection and recognition of our potential, we can welcome everything that comes our way—challenges and victories, pleasures and pains—as part of the magic, mystery, and beauty of life.

The *Healing Smile* revitalizes our life because it guides us to integrate our attention and our intention. This all-encompassing smile has the power to reveal a dynamic inner peace that changes how we perceive the world, including others and ourselves. From this inner peace, we can appreciate the preciousness of life within any situation, pleasant or unpleasant.

As an expression of inner unconditional love, the *Healing Smile* entices us to trust life. This trust paves the path of nonviolence, an essential principle common to all healing and spiritual traditions. Through love, openness, and acceptance towards the world, others and ourselves, we can find a sincere path to healing, friendship, peace, and happiness for ourselves and for those around us.

Even though the *Healing Smile* is one single practice, we will divide it into a sequence of four sections. The four-section sequence guides us to shine our loving smile from the more external to the more internal: starting with our surroundings, to the surface of our body, to the inside of our body, and, finally, to the union of these three spaces into one experience of blissful being. Dividing the practice into these four sections allows us to fully experience and integrate the benefits of our practice. Because these four sections lead from one to the other, they should be practiced in the order they are presented. As with all the other practices in this book, it is recommended that practitioners dedicate two weeks to each of the sections.

During the *Healing Smile* practice, we visualize a beautiful shining sun that bathes us with loving, healing light. Ideally, we practice the *Healing Smile* sitting on a chair and we imagine this sun shining light down from about three feet above the crown of our head—the length of our arm stretched upwards. The directions for each of the sections assume that we practice sitting on a chair. But it is also possible to practice the *Healing Smile* in any other position.

It is important to remember that the *Healing Smile* is not a social smile or a good manners smile. When cultivated after embracing the present moment and engaging in conscious breathing, the *Healing*

Smile is a loving and unpretentious smile that flows from the seed of pure perfection within the core of our universal being. Because the *Healing Smile* flows from the core of our universal being, when we shower ourselves with it, we cannot but reconnect ourselves with the essence and source of all life. The *Healing Smile* meditation is truly an exceptional practice for personal healing and awakening that contains all the layers of the path of self-development and realization.

For a guided version of the *Healing With The Smile* meditations go to:
www.joyfulheartinstitute.com/healing-now

PRACTICE
"SMILE AROUND YOU—
LIKE THE SUN FROM ABOVE"

"If you change the way you look at things,
the things you look at change."
~Wayne Dyer

In this first section of the *Healing Smile* we transform the space where we are into a universe replete with healing, restorative, and transformative qualities. From there, we expand these same virtuous qualities into the world and our life at large. As we practice, our inner declaration is, "Life is infinitely abundant. Infinite positive resources surround me. I have access to what I need and want to live a healthy, loving, joyful, and wakeful life."

Transforming our perception of the world around us is a crucial step in our healing journey because it refreshes what we consider possible for our own life. From this renewed perception, we can easily align the story we tell ourselves about our lives and our world with our profound desire for happiness and well-being.

Smile Around You—Like the Sun From Above reminds us that we can accelerate our healing and refine our well-being by mentally praising positive aspects of our surroundings, our current projects, and our dreams for our life. *Smile Around You—Like the Sun From Above* also reminds us that thriving is easier when we focus on what we want to experience in our surroundings instead of focusing on what we dislike about our surroundings. Instead of succumbing to emotional drama or ruminating on past trauma, the *Healing Smile* encourages us to connect with the love and wisdom that surrounds us.

Figure 2.1

Feeling the healing smile like sunshine around us.

DIRECTIONS

1. Sit comfortably with your back relaxed but straight and the soles of the feet fully flat on the ground to help you feel rooted on the Earth.
2. Take three relaxing breaths. Feel present in the moment and the place. Feel your mind calm and the body at ease.
3. Imagine a beautiful, large, radiant sun three feet above your head—about an arm's length.
4. Smile to this sun with a soft, grateful smile. As the sun receives your smile, its light expands and shines in all directions.
5. Imagine the shining light descending and expanding around you, extending across all space and in all directions: from above your head to your front and your back, to your left and your right, and then below you, going deep into the Earth.
6. As the light expands around and beyond you, imagine that it shines on the objects and circumstances around you, purifying and transforming the space where you are into a beautiful, vibrant, healing, abundant place.
7. Imagine also the shining healing light from the sun above you shining on all your personal projects and family members, filling them with virtues and positive elements that help them thrive.
8. Once you feel that the healing light shines on all your surroundings and your life at large, let go of any visualization and simply remain in the feeling of being immersed in the healing light that surrounds you. Relish the wonderful sun smiling back at you and your life.

- Awakening healing energy around us by generating positive emotions about our environment.
- Changing how we feel by changing how we view our surroundings.
- Letting go of tension and fear by connecting with a different way to perceive our world.
- Awakening creative energy for our personal projects and dreams.
- Transforming spaces to promote well-being and success.

PRACTICE INSIGHTS

Through the practice of *Smile Around You—Like the Sun From Above*, we cultivate a new way of seeing the world around us. Instead of perceiving endless chains of limitations and problems, we awaken into the certainty that every situation contains boundless potential for personal growth and enjoyment.

What does this have to do with healing? Many of our health issues arise from the stress-causing perceptions that the world, others, and ourselves are incomplete, difficult, problematic, and impure. Out of learned habit, we often label what we experience outside of us as problems and what we experience inside of us as traumas and illnesses.

While it is true that life presents us with challenges, it is also true that these challenges are the source of our personal growth. Challenges are like the resistance weights that strengthen our muscles at the gym. Challenges by themselves are neither good nor not good; it's we who label them as such based on how they make us feel.

Transforming our view of the world also transforms our understanding of who we are and how we experience ourselves. When we perceive potential for growth in every situation, we can feel calm, kind, and clear instead of impatient, resentful, and doubtful.

By letting the sun of the *Healing Smile* shine all around and beyond us, we no longer need to perceive the external world as the root of our challenges. Instead, we can choose to use everything we experience in daily life as a reminder to kindle love in our heart toward others and ourselves. Moment by moment, this new perspective enables us to recognize our healing process as part of our spiritual path.

By choosing to perceive our life from a positive vantage point, we stop demanding that the world fit our agenda to make us happy. Free from perceiving ourselves as a victim, our life becomes simpler and more enjoyable. Instead of living in fear and tension, we can choose to live with joy and excitement. Then, because the minds of all beings share a common basis, through our practice of *Smile Around You—Like the Sun From Above*, we are also planting powerful seeds of positive healing energy that extend beyond us to benefits all beings and situations.

PRACTICE
"SMILE ON YOURSELF—
LIKE THE SUN ON YOUR SKIN"

In the second section of the *Healing Smile*, we soften and regenerate the surface of our body and the tissues just under it—emphasizing our face, our neck, our shoulders, our arms, and our legs. Softening and regenerating the surface of our body has an overall deep healing effect because it relaxes tension and enhances the flow of vital force throughout our whole body.

Our body is the grail that holds our spirit. Regardless of all possible challenges our body might experience or what we might dislike about our body, it is always best to feel great appreciation towards our body. For this reason, as we practice *Smile On Yourself— Like the Sun On Your Skin*, our inner declaration is, "I appreciate and love my body. My body is the perfect guesthouse for my spirit to experience life in all its variety."

This deep appreciation towards our body implies special gratitude towards our parents and family—thanks to whom we have the chance to be alive. Also, if one believes that there is a divine awareness that is the source of our life, expressing gratitude towards our body is one of the highest possible forms of prayer.

Because of its softening and regenerating power on the surface of our body, *Smile On Yourself—Like the Sun On Your Skin* strengthens our immunity, because the energy field that surrounds our physical body is our first layer of immunity. Even though this outer energetic field emanates from our inner core, we can strengthen it through smiling and visualizing our surface and surroundings as shiny and vibrant.

Figure 2.2

Feeling the healing smile like sun rays on us.

1. Sit comfortably with your back relaxed but straight and the soles of the feet fully flat on the ground to help you feel rooted down to the Earth.

2. Take three relaxing breaths. Feel present in the moment and the place. Feel your mind calm and the body at ease.

3. Imagine a beautiful, large, radiant sun three feet above your head—about an arm's length.

4. Effortlessly and with gratitude smile to this sun. As the sun receives your smile, its light expands and shines in all directions.

5. At once, feel immersed in the healing light that surrounds you, as in the previous section, *Smile Around You—Like the Sun From Above*. Abide for a few breaths in the sensation of presence, wakefulness, openness, and stability.

6. Return to the image of the sun above your head. Again, smile to it with gratitude. As the sun receives your smile, its light shines down on you as if you were in a wonderful shower of healing light.

7. Begginig at the crown of your head, imagine the healing light spreading down the surface of your body. As your body relaxes, feel how all the cells of your skin heal and rejuvenate. Spend as much time as you need to in each area.

8. Start at the crown, scalp, and hair. Then, move down to the face—forehead, eyes, nose, cheeks, lips, ears—and to the back of the head, neck, and throat area. Continue feeling how the warmth of your smile awakens the healing potential of those areas.

9. Continue to the shoulders and then to the upper and lower arms until reaching the tips of the fingers.

10. Continue to the chest, breast, and abdomen.

11. Move to the upper, middle, and lower back. Next move down to the waist, to the buttocks, genital area, and the legs, until you reach the toes.

12. You can repeat steps 6 to 11 as many times as you feel like.

13. To finish, bring your attention to the area behind the navel, and breathe naturally from there as your center, resting in a state of openness and well-being.

HEALING BENEFITS

- Relieving tension and pain from neck, shoulders, and back.
- Improving blood circulation, lowering blood pressure, increasing vital energy, and strengthening immunity.
- Changing how we relate to ourselves by sending love to our body.
- Developing resilience to others' opinions about us.
- Boosting self-confidence, performance, and the ability to connect with others.

PRACTICE INSIGHTS

Our precious human body is an expression of divine love and the vehicle of our consciousness in this lifetime. When we smile on ourselves with joy, love, and gratitude, we soften negative and self-destructive judgments of our physical body and, therefore, of ourselves.

Smiling on ourselves with love is incompatible with demeaning thoughts such as "I'm fat" or "I'm ugly." As light dispels darkness, through practicing *Smile On Yourself—Like the Sun On Your Skin* we relate to our physicality in a loving and appreciative way. This self-love that transforms how we relate to ourselves is an unmistakable source of healing and goodness in our life.

Smile On Yourself—Like the Sun On Your Skin helps us realize and transform how we perceive ourselves in the world. Through our

PRACTICE
"SMILE INSIDE OF YOU—
LIKE THE SUN FROM THE INSIDE"

In the third section of the *Healing Smile*, we move deeper into our body to connect with our organs and glands. In healing and meditation practice, we regard each of our organs and glands for their emotional and mental functions aside from their commonly known anatomical forms and functions.

The main physical, emotional, and mental traits of major organs in good health are as follows (organs are listed in the order based on the energetic cycle within the body according to Traditional Chinese Medicine):

Lungs: *Physically* regulate breathing and elimination of toxins through exhalation and spread vital force throughout the body; *emotionally* support openness towards life, strengthen courage, and allow us to flow with changes without feeling stuck or attached; and *mentally* support clear and honest communication, making us receptive to the essence of life.

Large Intestine: *Physically* promotes elimination of waste, nourishes vital force, and strengthens immunity; *emotionally* allows us to let go and to see new possibilities in challenging situations; and *mentally* supports clarity by dispersing coarse thinking.

Stomach: *Physically* prepares food for digestion and strengthens our limbs; *emotionally* helps us process experiences and promotes centered, peaceful emotions; *mentally* grounds our creative mind to support our personal vision and helps integrate all mental functions.

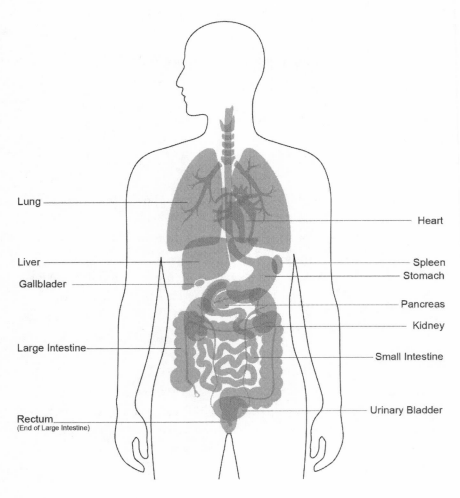

Lung

Heart

Liver

Spleen

Gallblader

Stomach

Pancreas

Kidney

Large Intestine

Small Intestine

Rectum
(End of Large Intestine)

Urinary Bladder

Figure 2.3

Internal organs.

Spleen: *Physically* promotes transformation and transportation of nutrients from digestive system to the rest of the body. Supports immunity by filtering blood and breaking down red blood cells; *emotionally* gives us stability by helping us feel grounded; *mentally* supports intellectual reasoning and promotes mental clarity by overcoming old patterns.

Heart: *Physically* pumps blood to supply nourishment, remove toxins, and regulates body temperature; *emotionally* balances all emotions and promotes love and joy; *mentally* coordinates all mental functions and maintains self-awareness.

Small Intestine: *Physically* regulates digestion of food and absorption of nutrients. Supports whole body immunity; *emotionally* helps integrate experiences and discard what is not useful; *mentally* supports sorting of useful ideas.

Urinary Bladder: *Physically* collects and holds urine; *emotionally* supports patience and composure and gives us strength to move forward; *mentally* allows us to look deeper into the essence of what we experience.

Kidneys: *Physically* filter the blood to eliminate toxins through urine and regulate mineral balance; *emotionally* promote perseverance and give us the ability to adapt; *mentally* store our inherited personal potential, connect us with essential wisdom beyond thinking and intellectual reasoning.

Gallbladder: *Physically* stores bile to assist with fat digestion; *emotionally* gives us courage to follow our insights; *mentally* supports making clear and firm decisions.

Liver: *Physically* filters our blood to cleanse and protect our body, breaks down chemicals to be eliminated, and metabolizes drugs; *emotionally* promotes kindness and flexibility; *mentally* helps develop personal vision, supports good judgment, and supports growth towards our spiritual goals.

The main physical, emotional, and mental traits of major glands in good health are as follows:

Uterus and prostate gland: *Physically* assist reproduction and elimination of toxins; *emotionally* provide a sense grounding, safety, and stability and also support our ability to nurture others and ourselves; *mentally* provide ability to stay on track with the essential aspects of our life and our projects.

Testicles and ovaries: *Physically* assist reproduction and development of physical traits; *emotionally* support harmonious relationships with self and others; *mentally* promote creativity and desire for change and variety.

Adrenals: *Physically* produce hormones to regulate metabolism, immunity, blood pressure, and stress response; *emotionally* help us recognize our uniqueness within our community; *mentally* provide enthusiasm and clear vision for our life plans.

Pancreas: *Physically* releases enzymes to promote digestion in small intestine and produces hormones to regulate sugar balance in body; *emotionally* supports our ability to enjoy life and digest experiences; *mentally* grounds the creative mind to support personal vision and helps integrate all mental functions.

Thymus: *Physically* plays a fundamental role in our immunity; *emotionally* awakens inner joy and promotes unconditional love to help us grow from "I to We"; *mentally* helps us mature and set up healthy boundaries.

Thyroid: *Physically* regulates metabolism, growth, development, and body temperature; *emotionally* balances our emotional system and supports our ability to clearly communicate our gifts for the benefit of our community; *mentally* encourages us to move past the intellect and experience who we are beyond the material world.

Pituitary: *Physically*, called the master gland because it sends hormones to regulate other glands and bodily functions like muscle and bone growth, stress regulation, metabolism, ovule and sperm production, and pain relief; *emotionally* encourages us to grow from "We to One"; *mentally* promotes seeing beyond appearances through clear insight and supports our intuition.

Pineal: *Physically* produces melatonin, regulates sleep patterns, and supports immunity and reproduction; *emotionally* allows us to embrace the experience of oneness that underlies all existence; *mentally* reveals our highest purpose in life.

In *Smile Inside of You—Like a Sun From the Inside*, we acknowledge our organs and glands and boost their three levels of function—physical, emotional, and mental. Shining a loving smile of gratitude on our organs and glands awakens them to their original blueprint for well-being.

When our organs and glands are reminded of their state of natural well-being, they remember how to effortlessly work together to help us detoxify, recharge, regenerate, and rejuvenate at all levels. As a result of this inner harmony, we can savor a state of blissful presence that pervades our body, emotions, and mind. To guide our organs and glands towards their natural state of well-being, our mental statement is, "I love myself, I enjoy myself. I feel complete, here and now."

Because this section requires more detailed instructions, the practice steps are titled according to the organs and areas they address. If you don't know exactly how to locate any of the organs or glands mentioned (e.g. the pineal gland located in the brain) don't worry. Simply smile to the large area—the brain in this case. The healing power of your smile will permeate the area and reach where it needs to reach.

1. Sit comfortably with your back relaxed but straight and the soles of the feet fully flat on the ground to help you feel rooted down to the Earth.
2. Take three relaxing breaths. Feel present in the moment and the place. Feel your mind calm and the body at ease.
3. Imagine a beautiful, large, radiant sun three feet above your head—about an arm's length.
4. Effortlessly and with gratitude smile to this sun. As the sun receives your smile, its light expands and shines in all directions.
5. At once, feel immersed in the healing light that surrounds you, as in the previous section, *Smile Around You—Like the Sun From Above*. Abide for a few breaths in the sensation of presence, wakefulness, openness, and stability.
6. Return to the image of the sun above your head. Again, smile to it with gratitude. As the sun receives your smile, its light shines down on you as if you were in a wonderful shower of healing light.
7. Starting from the crown of your head, imagine the healing light spreading down the surface of your body. As your body relaxes, feel how all the cells of the surface of your skin heal and rejuvenate. Spend as much time as you need to in each area.

8. *Smile to your brain, spine, and nervous system:*
    a. Imagine the healing light entering through the crown of your head into your brain, reaching deep into every brain cell.
    b. Send a special smile of gratitude to your pineal and pituitary glands in the center of your head.

110

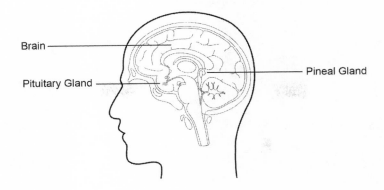

Figure 2.4

Smiling to the brain and main glands in the head.

  c. Once your brain is overflowing with healing light, let your smile spread into the spinal column and to the thousands of miles of nerves that reach every single cell of your body.

  d. As you would see sun rays enter through a window and shine into a room, visualize at once your body filled with small pathways shining with healing light.

9. *Smile to your face, neck, and throat:*

  a. Imagine the healing light entering your eyes, ears, sinuses, nose, mouth, teeth, tongue, and down the throat into the thyroid and parathyroid glands.

  b. Dedicate an extra healing smile to your thyroid and parathyroid glands since they play a crucial role in regulating metabolism, and to your thymus gland, essential for your immune system function.

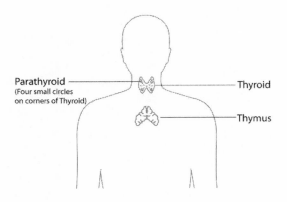

Figure 2.5

Smiling to the thyroid, parathyroid and thymus glands.

10. *Smile to your heart and cardiovascular system:*
   a. Imagine the healing light entering the upper chest. Smile to the thymus gland, essential for immunity.
   b. Imagine the healing light surrounding and filling the heart with gratitude for pumping constantly to keep you alive.
   c. Visualize the light cleansing the major veins and arteries that come in and out from the heart. Imagine how the healing light travels from your heart through all the thousands of miles of blood vessels across your body.
   d. With the healing light of your smile traveling through all your blood vessels, imagine all your blood is purified.
   e. Imagine each red and white blood cell in your blood receiving healing light while toxins and stale vital energy disappear like smoke in the air, and all tissues are refreshed and rejuvenated.

11. *Smile to your lungs:*
    a. Imagine the healing light entering the lungs. Smile at them with gratitude and love.
    b. First feel the right lung, next the left lung.
    c. From the shoulder to the bottom of the rib cage, imagine the healing light flooding, cleansing, and rejuvenating all cells.
    d. Feel the incoming breath refreshing the lungs and the outgoing breath taking away old toxins.

12. *Smile to your liver and gallbladder:*
    a. Imagine the healing light entering the right upper side of the abdomen, underneath the bottom of the rib cage. Bring the healing light to the liver, which is constantly working to filter the blood and produce hundreds of metabolic processes for your body and mind to work properly. The liver is quickly affected by stress, technology overuse and lack of proper rest, so smile at it with immense loving gratitude. Next, imagine the healing nectar surrounding and entering the gallbladder, the small bile sack attached to the liver that supports digestion. Spend a few breaths bathing both of these organs with your Healing Smile.

13. *Smile to your stomach, spleen, pancreas, and intestines:*
    a. Imagine the healing light descending from the mouth to the esophagus, shining into the solar plexus, and entering the stomach.
    b. Moving to the left upper side of the abdomen, underneath the bottom of the rib cage, guide the healing light to the spleen and pancreas. Smile to your stomach, spleen, and pancreas with gratitude and love. They are fundamental to the strength of your digestion, energy level, and immunity.

c. Direct the smile downward into the small intestine; it helps absorb nutrients and to discard what we can't really use. Move the smile into the large intestine, from where the waste is going to be eliminated.

d. Imagine your Healing Smile as a hose that from the inside of the intestines washes off old gunk and waste that is stuck there, leaving clean, healthy, and balanced tissues behind.

14. *Smile to your kidneys, adrenals and urinary system:*
    a. Imagine the healing light entering the mid and lower back area.
    b. With love and gratitude, first smile to the right kidney and then to the left kidney. Your kidneys are constantly filtering toxins from the blood to discard them through the urine. Also, express gratitude to your kidneys for regulating blood pressure and keeping minerals in balance.
    c. Send an extra smile to the adrenals, two triangle shaped glands above the kidneys, that produce stress-regulation and inflammation-control hormones.
    d. Move the healing smile down the ureters into the bladder and then out to the urethra. This smile is especially important for females who tend to be more prone to urinary tract infections.

15. *Smile to your genitals and reproductive organs:*
    a. Imagine the healing light entering the lower abdomen.
    b. Many physical, emotional, and mental issues, for both women and men, are connected to the reproductive organs and genitals, especially if there has been trauma due to abuse or sexual frustration. So bathe all these areas with great love.

Praise for *Dancing in the Dash*

"With special resonance for this moment in our country's history, Lauri, a friend of many years, shares a creative and compelling portrait of a Black woman making her mark, while handling her personal and professional lives with grace. Her story is a compelling testament to the transcendence of resolve, perseverance and resilience across generations of an American family."

—**Ambassador Susan E. Rice,**
former US national security advisor

"From private dinners with revolutionaries and heads of state to marathon strategy sessions with presidents and diplomats, Lauri Fitz-Pegado walks gracefully as a citizen of the world. Bolstered by a childhood of love and privilege, her personal quest for excellence created a launching pad for a life of purpose, impact, and adventure. At moments of inevitable grief and heartache, she drew sustenance from deeply cultivated friendships and her early training as a dancer. *Dancing in the Dash* will challenge us all to do more and will inspire young women to dream and dare to make a difference."

—**A'Lelia Bundles,**
author of *On Her Own Ground:
The Life and Times of Madam C. J. Walker*

"Lauri Fitz-Pegado shares her captivating life story with an honesty, insightfulness, and humanity that makes her book inspired and inspiring. Truly a 'page-turner' from start to finish."

—**Mavis Staines,**
artistic director and CEO, Canada's National Ballet School

"Lauri-Fitz-Pegado's *Dancing in the Dash* provides an interesting peek inside the development of a performing artist in a challenging time."

—Virginia Johnson,
artistic director, Dance Theatre of Harlem

"Secretary Ron Brown was a singularly impressive figure, and in his time at the Commerce Department gathered the most remarkable, enthusiastic, and diverse group of young colleagues I ever had the pleasure of meeting in my time as ambassador. Lauri was not just a part, but a key formal and informal leader of this group. I am so pleased that she has decided to present this collection of moments and memories from her life and career, not only because it is a record of history but because it is a hugely enjoyable work of literature. I hope that through the book she will continue to inspire, entertain, and teach, as she has done all her life."

—Dr. Miomir Zuzul,
founder of Dubrovnik International University,
former ambassador of Croatia
to the United Nations and the United States,
and former minister of foreign affairs of Croatia

"Lauri and I met through our mutual time in the private sector and soon discovered our shared views on diversity and inclusion. I was unaware, however, how complex and fascinating her life and career had been until I read this brilliantly written memoir. At this moment when racism is at the center of debate and discussion in the US, her life story provides valuable insights not often addressed or understood."

—Peter Woicke,
a former managing director of the World Bank
and CEO of the International Finance Corporation

Made in the USA
Middletown, DE
24 February 2024

49719040R00172

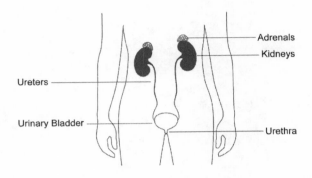

Figure 2.6

Smiling to the kidneys, adrenals and urinary system.

c. Women: imagine the healing light surrounding and entering the ovaries and descending to the fallopian tubes, into the uterus and the vagina.

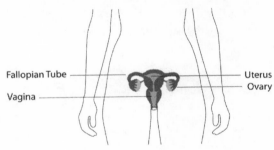

Figure 2.7

Smiling to the female reproductive system.

d. Men: imagine the healing light surrounding and entering the sperm vesicles and descending to the prostate gland, testicles, and penis.

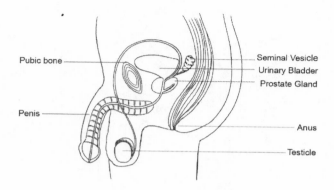

Pubic bone

Penis

Seminal Vesicle
Urinary Bladder
Prostate Gland

Anus

Testicle

Figure 2.8

Smiling to the male reproductive system.

16. You can repeat steps 8 to 15 as many times as you need.
17. To finish, bring your attention back to the area behind the navel and breathe naturally from there. Rest in a state of openness and well-being that radiates from all your inner organs and glands to the tips of fingers and toes, filling up all your inner space.

HEALING BENEFITS

- Improving the function of all our inner organs and glands.
- Increasing our vitality and strengthening our immunity.
- Opening the inner pathways for circulation and increasing communication among our organs.
- Rejuvenating our body and our mind. Balancing our emotions.
- Connecting with the inner source of healing. Increasing our self-esteem.

As an expression of love, the *Healing Smile* extends in two directions: outward towards the world and others, and inward towards our life and ourselves. Both directions are essential for our healing and well-being. Yet, because deep inside, it is easier for most of us to feel love towards others than towards ourselves, *Smile Inside of You—Like a Sun From the Inside* offers us an excellent way to love and heal ourselves.

The *Healing Smile* is one of the core practices of healing meditation because self-love is the core of our healing and well-being. Far from narcissism, vanity, or selfishness, self-love is the healthy expression of alignment between our worldly and divine identities. Like the proverb says, "Be humble for you are made of earth. Be noble for you are made of stars."

In contrast to what often happens during conventional psychological therapy or counseling, our healing process is not based on talking about what is wrong with us or what we are lacking. Instead, *Smile Inside of You—Like a Sun From the Inside* stems from the certainty that our essence is joyful and blissful wakefulness.

We will know that our practice is working when we feel physically better and have more energy. We will also know our practice is working when we depend less and less on external approval to feel good about ourselves.

The *Healing Smile* is primarily about increasing self-love, not about fighting disease. Still, as self-love increases, we realize that emotions like fear and anger can be leading contributors to illness. Even though we may think that the origin of disturbing emotions is external—what someone did to use or said to us, for example—the real cause is often the inner disconnection from our divine identity and the fear caused by not remembering who we really are. Over time, through the practice of the *Healing Smile*, we become more interested in looking inside for solutions than looking outside for people and situations to blame. As a result, we strengthen our emotional immunity and emotional maturity.

Smile Inside of You—Like a Sun From the Inside helps us heal from the illness of being affected by others' negative opinions and indifference. We heal because we reconnect with our joyful essence—not because we don't care about others. Indeed, connecting to this joyful essence allows to care more for others as well. From our joyful essence, we appreciate, enjoy, and love ourselves. The more we appreciate, enjoy, and love ourselves, the more we appreciate, enjoy, and love everyone else, regardless of how they behave towards us.

PRACTICE
"MERGING THE SPACES—
UNITING THE SMILES"

In the fourth and last section of the *Healing Smile*, our three smiles—external, surface, and internal—blend into one single, boundless field of wakeful being. As we rest in this state of boundless being, the solid feeling of our body and our world softens and dissolves. Our thoughts and our intentions also soften and dissolve. Simply abiding in open, unconfined awareness, we release any efforts to visualize or imagine anything at all.

Instead of using a mental statement, as we used in the three previous sections of the *Healing Smile*, we merely abide in the sublime experience of boundless being. With nothing to do and nobody to do it, being here is enough.

In the effortless union of our inner and outer experiences of being, we come to know our awareness as the light of lights, the universal consciousness that pervades and perceives all that is.

From a universal perspective, the light of lights is the fundamental essence of all beings and all worlds. As the essence of our individual and universal realities, the light of lights is the all-pervasive self-awareness life has of itself as it manifests in endlessly changing individual forms.

From a personal perspective, the light of lights is our individual awareness. As it condenses in the heart of each of us, the light of lights sparks our individual "I am" experience. Through the power of our senses, the light of lights activates our personal consciousness to perceive itself separate from the rest of the world—while, of course, at the same time our personal consciousness remains connected to the rest of the world since they share the same essence.

Beyond all form and thought, the light of lights is the foundation of all form and thought. Beyond we, you, and I, the light of lights is the oneness from where all duality and differentiation arises. As we read in the ancient Indian Upanishads:

"This boundless awareness,
That is you—the universe—and resides in your heart,
Needs no other light to illumine itself.
It is self-luminous. It is pure.
It is the one light, the light of lights.
All material objects, such as houses, rivers and forests,
Are illumined by the sun.
But the light that illumines the sun is the light of your heart.
The sun does not shine within your heart,
Nor the moon or the stars, nor the flames of the fire.
Yet, when your heart shines, everything shines after it;
By the light of your heart—the light of lights—
Everything is lighted."

And yet, even though we are the light of lights, the very essence of this whole universe, at the end of our practice, we must return to our daily activities. For this reason, after practicing *Merging the Spaces—Uniting the Smiles*, it is especially important to reawaken our physicality. To accomplish this, we tap softly but firmly on our head, face, chest, abdomen, back, arms, and legs with the palms of our hand. In this way, the experience of universality from our practice can enrich our view of who we are yet our mind and our body can come back to our daily life firm, present, and clear.

DIRECTIONS

1. Become aware of the radiant space around you, as you practiced in the first section of the *Healing Smile, Smile Around You—Like the Sun From Above*.

2. Become aware of the radiant space within you, as you

practiced in the third section, *Smile Inside of You—Like the Sun From the Inside*.

3. Feel how the healing light around you and inside of you is one and the same.

4. Connect with the healing light on your surface, as you practiced in the second section, *Smile on Yourself—Like the Sun On Your Skin*. Feel how this light is the same as the outer and inner healing light.

5. Smiling with love, from the crown of your head moving down towards your fingers and your toes, feel how the vibrant surface of your body melts. As your surface melts, the healing lights and the three spaces they occupy—the space around you, the space inside you, and your surface space—merge into a sensation of well-being, inner peace, and oneness.

6. Repeat steps 1 to 5 as many times as you would like.

7. Rest in loving, wakeful joy for a few minutes.

8. When you are ready to end your practice, softly bring your attention to your lower abdomen, in the space between the navel and the spine. Feel the sensation of well-being, inner peace, and oneness, collecting there and from there emanate back to the rest of your body and mind.

9. To finish, rub your hands together until they are warm. Then, gently rub your head, face, arms, chest, abdomen, and legs to revitalize your body and bring your mind back to your day. Make sure to maintain the shiny state of openness and well-being.

HEALING BENEFITS

- Deeply relaxing our body and our mind, facilitating blood circulation and energy flow through the whole body.

- Connecting us with the fundamental source of healing and well-being.
- Giving us energetic cohesion and improving immunity.
- Empowering us to follow what we know is right for us.
- Reminding us of our identity beyond our physical body and personal story.

PRACTICE INSIGHTS

Due to the constraints of ordinary perception and cultural paradigms, most of us have a view of who we are and what life is that is limited by the characteristics of our physical world. Even when we talk about spirituality or afterlife, our reasoning tends to be limited by our unsettled minds. Yet without a doubt, we are more that we can touch, see, feel, and think.

To helps us remember and experience that the light of lights is our essential nature, *Merging the Spaces—Uniting the Smiles* leads us to the gradual recognition of subtler and more expansive aspects of being. These subtler aspects are not something we imagine, create, or force in any way. These subtler aspects are always present in us, although we are not aware of them because we are used to focusing on denser aspects of our being, such as our physical body, our thoughts, and our emotions.

These deeper and more refined layers of being are always present in us yet we cannot perceive them, in the same way we cannot see the bottom of a lake during a storm, but once the storm passes and the waters calm, we can again see the bottom. While we are occupied with thought and emotional rollercoasters, we tend to remain unaware of the depth of our being. But once the superficial layers of our mind and emotions settle down, we start to experience who we are with clarity. The more we can allow our mind and emotions to settle, the clearer our blissful, essential nature becomes.

As individual beings, we are all born from the light of lights. Even when we forget where we come from, the light of lights remains our innermost essence and identity. When we can expand the limits of who we think we are beyond our body, our thoughts, our emotions, and our personal story, we start freeing ourselves from insecurities, limiting beliefs, and social conventions that condition and bind us. Therefore, remembering we are the light of lights is one of the highest healing experiences we can have.

As we rest in the light of lights, we let all our sensations, feelings, and thoughts dissolve into the experience of open being. Even our notions of well-being, happiness and joy dissolve. Resting with our awareness free from the mental concepts of who we are and how things should be, we move from intellectual knowledge into experiential wisdom.

What started as a loving smile that transformed our outer world and then regenerated our outer surface and finally healed and harmonized our inner body has now become the gateway to our boundless life. Naturally abiding in vibrant bliss and peace, we glimpse into our infinite potential for well-being, joy, and wisdom. Resting as the light of lights, we welcome our being as a constantly ever-new creation, life expressing itself as every moment, everywhere.

THE HEALING SMILE IN FOUR STANZAS

The following four stanzas express the essence of the Healing Smile practice. The four stanzas are not a practice to be repeated daily for two weeks as the other practices, even though you can if you wish. The four stanzas are a prelude to a state of effortless relaxation.

It is better to read the four stanzas slowly, letting the meaning of every sentence blossom in your experience of the present moment. You can read the four stanzas at once or simply choose one. After reading, remain resting in a comfortable position, letting your mind at ease without needing to visualize or imagine anything.

"With the body relaxed and soft, alive,
And the mind awake, present,
We feel the space that emanates from within
And expands in all directions.

In this experience of well-being,
Problems dissolve in their essence
As we recognize the simplicity of our being.

Light fills our body—the universe.
Our attention—self-awareness—
Rests in a natural joy.

All the cells of our body, our organs, and all our functions
Reach their maximum potential and state of health.
We feel well, light, conscious, happy, and optimistic.
This is the Healing Smile."

III

HEALING WITH SOUND AND COLOR

HEALING IS ABOUT GOOD VIBES

B oth ancient sages and modern scientists tell us that our body
is a vibrational entity inside a universe that is in constant
vibration. Whether it is the Bible stating that, "In the beginning
was the Word"—word being sound, sound being vibration—or
quantum physics telling us that the objects we perceive are made
up vortices of energy that are constantly spinning and vibrating,
ancient spiritual and modern scientific sources agree that the whole
universe and everything it contains are in constant motion.

All matter—solid, liquid, or gas—is made up of fields of
vibrating atoms that, like wobbly, spinning tops, radiate energy
as they move. Even objects that appear stationary and unwavering,
including your hands and this book, are made up of constantly
vibrating particles. The vibrational nature of our world also
includes sounds, feelings, and even thoughts—since it is through
vibrations that mental patterns and visualized images arise in our
mind.

The fact that our world is constantly vibrating has profound
implications for our healing meditation practice and our life as
a whole. Since our world and ourselves are essentially made up
of energy in constant motion, we can guide the direction of this
energy through our intention and attention. In guiding our
internal energies and the energies of our environment, we can
create a more enjoyable experience of being in the material world
that we perceive with our senses.

Our experience of the material world takes place mostly
through the vibrations of sound and color. Different sounds and
colors are the expression of different vibrations. Each of these
different vibrations has different qualities that affect our body and
mind in unique ways. Because sound and color have the ability to

quickly transform how we feel, they are essential tools in healing meditation.

Through observing nature along with meditating to still their minds and cultivating their insight, ancient sages and healing meditation practitioners realized that all our body parts and inner organs have unique healthy vibrations that correlate with specific sounds and colors. When we consciously make these sounds while we visualize their associated colors, our body parts and inner organs vibrate according to their original blueprint of well-being. The regular practice of observing these sounds and colors promotes a healthier, happier, and more fulfilling life because it helps us be in harmony with the balanced energies of our environment.

Sound has an immediate effect on all our systems—especially our nervous and circulatory systems—because it causes the cells of our body to vibrate in specific patterns. Combining sounds that we consciously produce with the rhythm of our breathing is one of the fastest ways to balance our being. Healing meditation uses sounds that create harmonious communication between the different aspects of our body, energy, and mind to promote healing, well-being, and personal growth.

As an expression of different wavelengths of light, color also has a profound effect on us. In healing meditation practice, we frequently imagine different color lights in combination with sound and breathing patterns. Using color lights as part of our practice has a profound effect on how we feel because the colors we see inside our mind are a reflection of the pure light of our awareness. This pure inner light connects us with a state of being beyond our physical body and the material world. Visualizing healing colors balances the vibration of our nervous system and connects our mind with our divine inner light, which is the divine inner light of all beings and all existence.

Because light waves travel at tremendous speed—186,000 miles per second—light bypasses reason and intellect, opening our body, energy, and mind to new healing and growth possibilities.

Since light dispels darkness, visualizing color can remove stagnation, improve mood, increase immunity, and stabilize well-being. The healing power of our inner light increases when we use golden white light. Visualizing golden white light reminds us of sunshine, which is essential to promoting overall well-being because sunshine increases energy levels, reduces inflammation, improves brain function, and supports immunity and detoxification.

For a guided version of the *Healing with Sound and Color* meditations go to:

www.joyfulheartinstitute.com/healing-now

PRACTICE
"LISTENING TO THE SOUND
OF OUR BREATH"

As we learned in *Healing With the Breath*, observing our breathing is a simple yet profound healing meditation. Now we modify this practice by maintaining our focus entirely on the sound of our breath as air comes in and out.

To help us understand this practice, it can be useful to imagine that we are by the ocean shore. Relaxing into the sound of the waves, we merge with the ocean's steady and firm yet ever-changing and effortless rhythm. As if listening to the ocean waves, listening to our breathing relaxes our whole body, soothes our emotions, and makes our mind feel spacious and content.

Listening To the Sound of Our Breath is a unique practice that helps us enrich our relationship with the vital force that enlivens our environment and us. Because it prompts us to blend our attention with the breath of life, listening to our breathing is a profoundly restorative practice that can renew our longevity at two levels—both our lifespan and our experience of the present moment:

- *Lifespan:* Some spiritual traditions believe that we are born with a certain amount of breaths as our lifespan. Because listening to our breathing naturally slows down the speed at which we breathe, this practice can help us enjoy a longer life.
- *Experience of the present moment:* By resting our attention on the sound of our breathing, we deepen our experience and understanding of the present moment

as something beyond time and space. As we refine our experience of the present moment, we gain depth of longevity in the boundless *now*.

DIRECTIONS

1. Sit or lie down comfortably.
2. Bring your attention to the place and moment where you are. Allow your mind to be at ease.
3. Take three relaxing breaths. Allow your body to soften.
4. For a few breaths, bring your attention to the flow of air coming in and out of your body.
5. Then, bring your attention to the sound of your breathing as the air comes in and out of your body.
6. Remain aware of the sound of your breathing, softly but attentively, for 3 to 30 minutes.

HEALING BENEFITS

- Relieving physical tension and pain.
- Improving absorption of nutrients and digestion of experiences.
- Connecting us to the flow of the breath of life and making our cells more receptive to the breath of life as nourishment.
- Relaxing our mind and harmonizing our nervous system.
- Giving us a broader perspective on life and promoting longevity.

PRACTICE INSIGHT

Listening To the Sound of Our Breath is a fundamental healing meditation practice that clears subtle blockages from our energy system. Clearing subtle blockages from our energy system benefits all aspects of our body and mind, stabilizing our meditation practice and providing us with more emotional freedom to enjoy life.

The essence of this practice is to simply remain aware of the sound of our breath. Maintaining a soft body and a relaxed, open mind helps us sustain mindfulness and prevents unnecessary tension or excessive focus. If we realize we have become distracted or tense, we simply return to the soothing sound of our breathing.

As we practice, it is important to notice the texture of our breathing sound. This texture, almost like a light friction, charges our breathing with healing energy that rejuvenates our physical and energetic bodies. At the beginning of our practice, our breathing might sound smooth. Yet, as we settle into the practice, we might realize that our breathing is actually chunky.

Listening closely to our breathing, we might notice subtle crackling sounds we have never heard previously. These sounds reflect energetic cysts within our energy channels and our mind, caused by the hardening of repetitive thoughts, limiting beliefs, and old traumas. Because these cysts hold the energetic memory of unprocessed past events and limiting beliefs, they tend to make our energy system vibrate in ways that can attract things to our life related to their contents.

As if polishing a mirror, by *Listening To the Sound of Our Breath*, we learn to recognize and resolve these cysts, gradually releasing subtler inner resistances within the conscious and subconscious layers of our mind. The clearer the surface of the mirror, the deeper our understanding of who we are and of how we can experience well-being and joy.

PRACTICE
"THE *AH* SOUND"

Ah is the natural sound we make when we find relief, comfort, or when we want to generate a sense of well-being. We often spontaneously make this sound when we taste nice food, sit after a long walk, encounter a solution for an issue, or try to release tension and frustration.

The practice of consciously making the "Ah" sound is a pleasant and efficient way to direct our body towards healing, to balance our emotions, and to awaken our mind. A soft, long "Aaaaahhhh" soothes our emotions and our mind because it reconnects us with an experience of relaxation and openness. As we feel more relaxed and open to life, our body softens and our feeling of well-being increases.

The main instruction for this practice is to breathe out making a soft "Ah" sound, as if sighing in joyful relief. As we exhale while making the sound "Ah," we smile to our body and feel a deep sense of relaxation as when we receive good news about something that had been causing us stress.

Before exhaling with the soft "Ah" sound, we prepare ourselves by consciously inhaling and then holding our breath in for a moment. This preparation is essential to make our practice efficient. We only hold our breath in for as long as it feels comfortable. This gentle pause before breathing out gives us time to collect our attention in our body. Once we feel the need to exhale, we release the air with a soft wave of relaxation while we make the sound "Ah."

In the same way an ocean wave reaches the shore, we follow our exhalation into a state of peaceful well-being by letting go of all tension. Without losing our awareness, we entice our body to relax following the sound "Ah," with special attention to the moments after having completed our exhalation. Being aware of the short breathing pauses after exhaling stabilizes our sense of joyful relief and promotes healing for our body and mind.

DIRECTIONS

1. Sit comfortably with your back straight and relaxed.
2. Bring your attention to the place and moment where you are. Allow your mind to be at ease.
3. Take three relaxing breaths. Allow your body to soften.
4. After your next inhalation, hold your breath for a brief moment. Then, purposely exhale making a soft "Aaaaahhhh."
5. Take a couple more regular breaths, without making the sound "Ah."
6. Then inhale again, hold the breath for a brief moment, and exhale while consciously producing a soft "Aaaaahhhh."
7. Repeat this sequence as many times as you want, ideally at least nine times.
8. To finish, rest in a state of relaxed, mindful presence for 3 to 30 minutes.

HEALING BENEFITS

- Releasing physical tension and promoting blood flow.
- Improving digestion and bowel movement.
- Signaling the body to move from a state of emergency and stress to a state of restoration and relaxation.
- Clearing our mind of worry, fear, and selfishness.
- Balancing the activity of the nervous system.

Chanting the "Ah" sound is a simple healing meditation practice that can greatly benefit our overall health by balancing our autonomic nervous system. Our autonomic nervous system has two main branches: sympathetic and parasympathetic. The sympathetic branch prepares our body for intense activity and triggers the emergency state known as fight-or-flight. The parasympathetic branch guides our body to relax, repair, and restore itself.

In an ideal state of health, the relationship between these two branches of our nervous system flows naturally: we spend most of our time in a parasympathetic state of relaxation, repair, and restoration, and we activate a sympathetic state to address demands for higher energy and more focused attention, such as moments of peak performance, emergencies, and threatening situations. The key to maintaining this healthy relationship between these two branches of our nervous system is that once the acute demands for higher energy are fulfilled, our nervous system returns to a state of relaxation.

Yet, because most of our lives are packed with activities that require great physical, emotional, and mental resources, our nervous systems are constantly on high-demand mode. This strenuous lifestyle where our nervous systems feel bombarded throughout the day causes us to suffer from an excess of sympathetic activity. Excess of sympathetic activity unavoidably leads to chronic stress, which negatively impacts our health. Directly or indirectly, chronic stress both causes and exacerbates nervous, digestive, allergic, inflammatory, hormonal, and cardiovascular disorders.

As an antidote to the habit of chronic stress, softly resounding "Ah" across our body has a profound balancing effect for our whole being. When we chant "Ah," as if sighing, we gently invite our body to switch from the tension caused from sympathetic stress to the loving warmth of parasympathetic relaxation.

Another important consideration to help us understand the value of this practice is that, in healing meditation, the "Ah" sound harmonizes our heart. We will learn about the different healing sounds for each organ later in this chapter, in the *Five Elements Healing Meditation* practice. For now, it is enough to know that the "Ah" sound has a special relationship with our heart. Also, within the context of healing meditation, it is important to realize that our heart is not just the organ that pumps our blood. In healing mediation, our heart is the house of our divine inner being. Therefore, as we softly chant—or sigh—the "Ah" sound, we allow our spirit to expand deeper into all aspects of our lives.

As our divine inner being expands further through the practice of the "Ah" sound, we can savor who we are when we are less conditioned by repetitive thoughts and limiting mental patterns. Through this clearer expression of our divine inner being into our daily experience, our mind can perceive and understand with more clarity how to find well-being, joy, and fulfillment in all situations.

PRACTICE
"CENTERING AND PURIFYING BREATHING
WITH SOUND AND COLOR"

*C*entering and Purifying Breathing With Sound and Color is a variation of the *Centering and Purifying Breathing* practice from chapter one. As noted in the practice insights for *Centering and Purifying Breathing*, alternated nostril breathing is one of the most important practices in this book because it profoundly benefits our body, emotions, and mind by balancing our brain and nervous system.

Centering and Purifying Breathing With Sound and Color presents two main changes from the previous version: first, instead of using our fingers to block our nostrils, we feel that we breathe in from the sole of one foot up to the head, and then we feel that we breathe down and out the other side our body; second, we add colors and sounds to the breathing pattern. These additions combine the power of breathing with healing sounds and colors. However, it is important to understand that both practices—the simpler method presented in chapter one and the more elaborate presented here—are equally wonderful healing meditation tools. We should not think that one is better than the other one. Instead, through our practice we just need to understand when to use one or the other method.

Centering and Purifying Breathing With Sound and Color starts by guiding us through the particular breathing pattern for this practice. Once we feel comfortable with the breathing pattern, the practice introduces colors and sounds for each side of our body.

Red and blue healing lights correspond to our male and female inner energies—our dynamic and receptive aspects of being.

The red and blue healing lights are also associated with two of our main energetic channels. These energetic channels connect with our nostrils and our brain—the right solar-fire and left lunar-water channels. Visualizing the red and blue healing lights within our body balances the polarity between our two fundamental energies, empowering our personality with a joyful, creative, and proactive self-confidence.

"Hreem" and "Shreem" are two healing sounds that promote personal healing and self-development. The vibrations of these two sounds have unique healing benefits for our body and mind: "Hreem" increases our energy and magnetism; it helps us develop focus, clarity, and motivation; and it provides warmth and purifies blockages from our energy channels. "Shreem" help us relax and feel at ease; it helps us balance our feelings and emotions; and it increases our creativity by opening our mind to subtler aspects of being—as, for example, through dreams—and helps us appreciate and enjoy the beauty of life. Allowing the vibrations of "Hreem" and "Shreem" blend within us can lead us to experience profound joy and bliss.

LEFT SIDE	RIGHT SIDE
Lunar – Water	Solar – Fire
Female	Male
Receptive – Feeling	Dynamic – Doing
Blue healing light	Red healing light
"Shreem"	"Hreem"

DIRECTIONS

1. Sit toward the edge of the chair, keeping your back straight but relaxed and your feet flat on the ground. If you prefer you can also practice lying down comfortably, elevating your knees with the help of a pillow to support your lower back.

2. Bring your attention to the place and moment where you are. Allow your mind to be at ease.
3. Take three relaxing breaths. Allow your body to soften.

Practicing the breathing pattern:

4. Bring your attention to the sole of your left foot.
5. From the sole of your left foot, breathe in upwards through the left side of your body to the left side of your brain, or as high as you comfortably can. (Fig. 3.1)
6. Before you start exhaling, bring your attention to the right side of your brain. From the right side of your brain, breathe out down the right side of your body to the sole of your right foot. (Fig. 3.2)

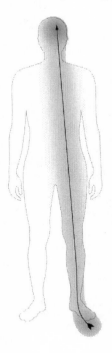
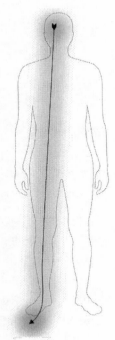

Figure 3.1
Breathing in and up left side of body.

Figure 3.2
Breathing out and down right side of body.

7. From the sole of your right foot—the same side you breathed out—breathe in upwards through the right side of your body to the right side of your brain. (Fig. 3.3)

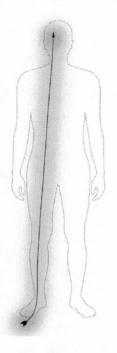 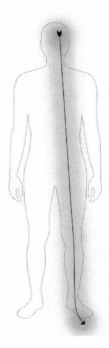

Figure 3.3
Breathing in and up right side of body.

Figure 3.4
Breathing out and down left side of body.

8. Before you start exhaling, bring your attention to the left side of your brain. From the left side of your brain, breathe out down the left side of your body to the sole of your left foot. (Fig. 3.4)
9. Steps 4 to 8 complete one cycle. Repeat this cycle at least three more times, or until you become used to the breathing pattern before proceeding to the next section.

Breathing the healing colors:

10. Bring your attention to the sole of your left foot.
11. From the sole of your left foot, breathe in blue-golden healing light. As you breathe in, the blue-golden healing light travels up the left side of your body to the left side of the brain, or as high as you comfortably can. The ascending light makes you feel healthy, present, relaxed, comfortable, and happy.
12. Before you start breathing out, imagine the ascending blue light moving from the left to the right side of your brain. As it moves from left to right, the healing light turns a red-golden color.
13. From the right side of your brain, breathe out red-golden light down towards you right foot. As you exhale, the red-golden healing light travels down the right side of your body and exits through the sole of your right foot to the center of the Earth. The descending light removes tension, disease, worries, and traumas from your body and mind.
14. When you need to inhale again, imagine fresh red-golden healing light ascending from the sole of your right foot—the same side it went out—to the right side of your brain. The ascending light makes you feel healthy, present, relaxed, comfortable, and happy.
15. Before you start breathing out, imagine the ascending red healing light moving from the right side of your brain to the left side. As it moves from right to left, the healing light turns a blue-golden color.
16. From the left side of your brain, breathe out blue-golden light going towards your left foot. As you exhale, the healing blue-golden light travels down the right side of your body and exits through the sole of your left foot to the center of the Earth. The descending light removes tension, disease, worries, and traumas from your body and mind.

Breathing the healing sounds:

17. Start inhaling up the left side imagining blue-golden healing light ascending from your left sole to your brain, as in the previous section. When you exhale, going down the right side, from your brain to your right foot, along with the red-golden healing light, make the sound "Hreem."

18. At a slow pace, inhale red-golden healing light up the right side, from your foot to your brain. When you exhale, going down the left side, from your brain to your left foot, along with the blue-golden healing light, make the sound "Shreem." This completes a cycle. Repeat 3 to 9 cycles.

Creating the self-luminous inner jewel:

19. Bringing your attention to the center of your abdomen, invite the blue and red healing lights to blend behind your navel. As the healing lights mix, they condense into a vibrating golden sphere that radiates rainbow healing light, well-being, and wisdom, filling your body and spreading beyond you in all directions. This is your self-luminous inner jewel.

20. As you inhale, feel that you are breathing in the finest universal healing energies of water and fire. These energies gather behind your navel to nourish your self-luminous inner jewel with universal harmony, creativity, joy, love, peace, and wisdom. As you exhale, the healing radiance of your self-luminous inner jewel shines from behind your navel across your body, radiating out from all the pores of your skin and all the orifices of your body—eyes, nose, ears, mouth, and lower orifices.

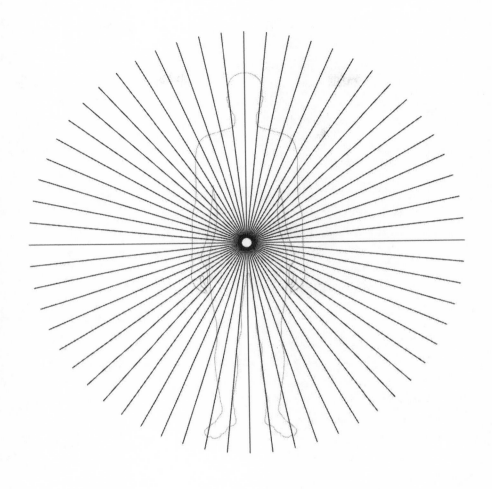

Figure 3.5
Creating the self-luminous inner jewel.

21. Abide in this pulsating experience of joyful radiance for as long as you want. To finish, gather all the virtues and lights back into the self-luminous inner jewel, and completely rest your mind for a few breaths to allow the healing energies to further integrate in your body and energy system.

22. Then, activate the intention that your self-luminous inner jewel will continue to shine from within, keeping your body, energy, and mind balanced, healthy, and clear, allowing you to become a beacon of harmony, creativity, joy, love, peace, and wisdom for all other sentient beings across all worlds.

HEALING BENEFITS

- Regaining energetic integrity and restoring vitality.
- Relieving one-sided physical and energetic imbalances.
- Calming the mind and balancing brain activity.
- Unblocking creative potential and activating creative processes.
- Developing self-love and self-reliance.

PRACTICE INSIGHTS

Centering and Purifying Breathing With Sound and Color is a practice that helps us restore a balanced flow of energy throughout our body, emotions, and mind. In general, many of our daily activities emphasize one side of our body. For example, most of the time we use the same hand to hold our phone, we sleep in the same position, and we sit with our legs crossed the same way. Also, emotionally and mentally, we tend to emphasize certain patterns, opinions, and beliefs. Repetitive movements, emotions, and mental patterns can cause an uneven flow of energy in our system. Over time, this uneven flow of energy can lead to physical ailments and to a hardening of our personality.

In *Centering and Purifying Breathing with Sound and Color*, we reestablish the even pulsation of our energy field by combining the flow of our breath with the visualization of color and the vibration of sound. Breathing the red and blue healing lights while softly chanting "Hreem" and "Shreem" harmonizes the energies of fire and water within our body and mind. This inner harmony of fire and water has profound implications for our healing and self-development journey, because our biological father and mother are embodiments of the universal energies of fire and water. Regardless of their personalities and how they have influenced us, our well-being is deeply connected to how we relate to our parents. How we feel about ourselves, how we relate to others, how we face our challenges, and how we enjoy our accomplishments are directly influenced by our ability to love and accept our parents for who they are. In other words, how we live our life is in great measure a reflection of our capacity to sincerely feel gratitude towards our parents.

Centering and Purifying Breathing With Sound and Color is an important practice that helps us harmonize our relationship with our biological parents by helping us discover and integrate balanced male and female energies within ourselves. The harmonious union of these two internal energies helps us move forward in life with confidence and optimism without seeking for external approval. By extension, our practice grounds us in a state of self-love that promotes openness and loving communication in our intimate relationships.

After awakening and harmonizing the energies of fire and water within us, it is ideal practice to blend them into one single essence behind our navel. Woven together through our breathing and visualization, these two energies blend into an inner self-luminous jewel that radiates self-reliance, calmness, well-being, and joy from the center of our abdomen. The integration of the essences of fire and water—the warmth of our inner sun and the coolness of our inner moon—ensures that their properties will continue to nourish us from the core of our being after we have completed our practice session.

Practicing *Centering and Purifying Breathing With Sound and Color* in a gentle, fluid, and enjoyable way helps us emphasize the healing, harmonizing, and transformative energies within ourselves. There is no need to make any special effort to balance our inner energies. Through regular practice, our inner fire and water will gradually balance each other, opening us to finer awareness of who we are.

As we practice, we visualize the healing lights moving up and down our body effortlessly, like a healing mist with exquisite temperature and sensation. When we breathe out, we feel tension, stress, and anything else that is not serving us leaving our body. If we are dealing with a health issue, we imagine the illness leaving our body as thick, dark energy that sinks to the center of the Earth. Once this thick, dark energy reaches the fire at the center of the Earth, we feel how the unhealthy energy is purified and transformed into fresh healing, golden light that returns to our body with our next inhalation.

Visualizing the unhealthy energy purified and transformed into fresh healing golden light helps us transform critical contributors to the illnesses and challenges we want to overcome. By transforming these root causes, we firmly plant the intention that the illnesses and challenges we are transforming resolve quickly and permanently. To strengthen the transformation of root causes, we welcome the positive opposite to whatever we are eliminating. For example, if we release disease, we inhale well-being; if we release fear, we inhale courage and inner peace; if we release anger, we inhale loving-kindness. Through this transformation, we rejuvenate ourselves by awakening our consciousness, freeing our creativity, and releasing our obsession with *doing* and instead learn to savor the joy of *being*.

PRACTICE
"FIVE ELEMENTS HEALING MEDITATION"

According to ancient healing and spiritual principles, Water, Wood, Fire, Earth, and Metal are the building blocks of life (Fig. 3.6). These five elements create, sustain, and ultimately recycle the universe and all its endless diversity. Everything we experience internally through our mind, as well as everything we perceive externally through our five senses, is the expression of these five elemental energies interacting with each other. The five elements are the basis of all phenomena, the substance of all things and processes—physical, energetic, mental, and spiritual.

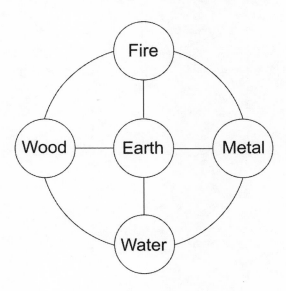

Figure 3.6
The five universal elements.

Element	Metal	Water	Wood
Main Organ	Lungs	Kidneys	Liver
Paired Organ	Large Intestine	Bladder	Gallbladder
Color	White	Dark Blue	Green
Sound	Ssss	Chuuu	Xeee
Virtues	Openness and good communication	Wisdom and perseverance	Kindness and flexibility
Imbalance	Sadness, worry, and attachment	Fear, shock, and lack of will power	Frustration, anger, and depression

Element	Fire	Earth	Fire
Main Organ	Heart	Spleen -Pancreas	Pericardium
Paired Organ	Pericardium	Stomach	San Jiao
Color	Red	Yellow	Pink
Sound	Aaahhh	Hooo	Heee
Virtues	Love and joy	Stability and acceptance	Self-love, caring intimacy, and harmonious relationships
Imbalance	Over-excitement, anxiety and hatred	Over-thinking, worry and melancholia	Self-aggression, inhibition and resentment

Through their insightful observation of energetic movements in nature and within their own bodies, healing meditation practitioners from the past realized that the same elemental energies found in our environment are present within us. As a physical manifestation of the energies of the five elements, each of our inner organs and their functions has a unique, healthy vibration that relates to the five elements through specific colors, sounds, and virtues. By using the colors, sounds, and virtues of the five elements as part of their daily routine of self-care, ancient healing meditation practitioners discovered that it was easier to live a healthy and joyful life.

Similar to the effect of watering and fertilizing plants, when we reconnect our organs with their elemental colors, sounds, and virtues, we nourish our personal vibration to help us thrive. By flooding our organs with the healing lights, sounds, and virtues of the five elements, we feel physically better, have more energy, experience more positive emotions, experience greater mental clarity, and have an easier time manifesting an abundant and joyful life.

It is helpful to begin on the Metal element since it connects with our lungs and breathing, which smooths the energy circulation in our body and frees energetic resources to address the other elements and organs. Once we complete the cycle of the five elements—Metal, Water, Wood, Fire, and Earth—we further harmonize the five elements by using a second layer of the Fire element, in this case related to the pericardium and *san jiao* organs. The *san jiao* is a specific organ within Eastern medicine that relates to the western hormonal system as well as the abdominal and chest cavities.

As we practiced in *Centering and Purifying Breathing With Sound and Color*, after we have flooded our organs with healing lights, sounds, and virtues of the five elements, we gather their healing energies behind our navel to nourish our self-luminous inner jewel. Creating and nourishing the inner jewel behind our navel stabilizes our physical, emotional, and mental well-being, providing us with clarity about how to make our life meaningful. With the sustained radiance of our inner jewel, we also become a calm source of joyful support for everyone with whom we come into contact.

1. Sit comfortably with your back straight and relaxed.
2. Bring your attention to the place and moment where you are. Allow your mind to be at ease.
3. Take three relaxing breaths. Allow your body to soften.

Harmonizing the Metal element:

4. Place your palms on your chest, over your lungs. Smile to your lungs as you would smile to a good friend you have not seen in long time. Thank your lungs for all their work. (Fig. 3.7)

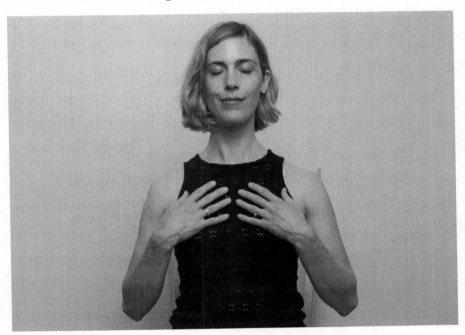

Figure 3.7
Connecting with our lungs.

5. As you continue to breathe naturally, observe how your lungs feel. Ask them if there is something you can do to make their work easier and help them feel better. Spend a few more breaths observing your lungs. Be receptive to any information your lungs offer you and anything else you sense about them.

6. As you continue smiling to your lungs, imagine that the essence of all healing energy and universal love manifests as beautiful white-golden light that pools around and inside your lungs. Imagine the white-golden light brings to your lungs whatever they need to cleanse them, to help them regain balance, and to improve their functioning at all levels.

7. As you exhale, make the sound "Sssssss" vibrate inside and around your lungs. The vibration of the sound mixes with the white-golden light, causing the light to intensify and expand. As you continue exhaling, the vibration of the "Sssssss" sound causes stagnant and unhealthy energy to leave your lungs. As you inhale again your lungs are filled with clean, healthy, and vibrant energy in the form of white-golden light.

8. Repeat the cycle of inhaling white-golden light and exhaling the "Sssssss" sound three times: the first time with normal volume, the second time whispered, and the third time silent but with clear internal sound.

9. Rest your hands on your lap and spend a few breaths feeling your happy lungs shining white-golden healing light.

10. Feel the healing light expanding into the large intestine—the paired organ of the lungs. Once your large intestine is overflowing with white-golden healing light, the light expands throughout your whole physical body and around it.

11. As the white-golden healing light continues shining inside and around you, feel the virtues of openness and good communication radiate throughout your being, dissipating sadness, worry, and attachment. Spend a few breaths feeling the virtues associated with your lungs.

12. Then let go of any visualization and simply rest for a few breaths until you feel ready to move to the next element. Steps 4 to 12 complete the section on the Metal element.

Harmonizing the other four elements:

13. Once you are ready to move to the next organ, repeat steps 4 to 12 following the sequence of the elements according to the chart on page 152. Repeat the same steps you followed for the Metal element (lung and large intestine), making sure you change the color of the light you inhale, the sound you vibrate, and the virtues you feel:

Water Element (the kidneys and urinary bladder): "Chuuu" sound; navy blue-golden light; the virtues of wisdom and perseverance, dissipating fear, shock, and lack of will power. (Fig. 3.8)

Wood Element (liver and gallbladder): "Sheeee" sound; green-golden light; virtues of kindness and flexibility, dissipating frustration, anger, and depression. (Fig. 3.9)

Fire Element (heart and small intestine): "Aaahhh" sound; red golden light; virtues of love and joy, dissipating over-excitement, anxiety, and hatred. (Fig. 3.10)

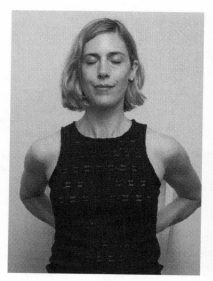

Figure 3.8
Connecting with our kidneys.

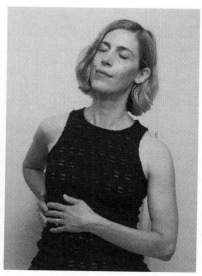

Figure 3.9
Connecting with our liver.

Figure. 3.10
Connecting with our heart.

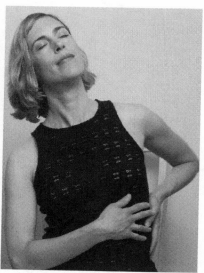

Figure. 3.11
Connecting with our spleen.

Earth Element (pancreas-spleen and stomach): "Huuu" (from the throat, like gargling) sound; orange golden light; virtues of stability and integrity, dissipating over thinking, worry, and melancholia. (Fig. 3.11)

14. Steps 4 to 13 complete one round of harmonization of the five elements. After completing this cycle one or more times, rest for a few breaths, enjoying the renewed well-being of your body and mind.

Harmonizing the san jiao:

15. Visualize your body surrounded by pink-golden light and inhale, bringing your hands above your head. (Fig. 3.12)
16. As you exhale, move your hands down towards your feet, making the healing sound "Heeee." The sound mixes with the pink-golden light, moving downwards, releasing from your body any remaining stale energy. As you inhale again, feel a profound sense of well-being and joy.
17. Repeat steps 15 and 16 three times.
18. Rest your hands on your lap and spend a few breaths feeling your body surrounded by exquisite pink-golden healing light. As the pink-golden healing light continues shining around you, feel the virtues of self-love, caring intimacy, and harmonious relations radiate throughout your being, dissipating self-aggression, inhibition, and resentment.

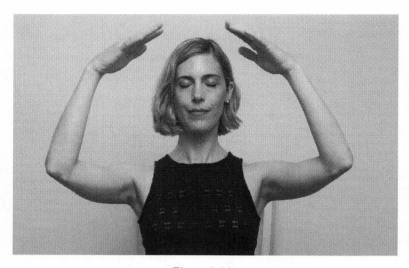

Figure 3.12

Bathing our whole body with
pink-golden healing light.

Nourishing your self-luminous inner jewel:

19. Mentally invite the lights and virtues of the five
elements to the area behind the navel to nourish your
self-luminous inner jewel with universal harmony,
creativity, joy, love, peace, and wisdom. As you exhale,
the healing radiance of your self-luminous inner jewel
shines from behind your navel across your body,
radiating out from all the pores of your skin and all
the orifices of your body—eyes, nose, ears, mouth, and
lower orifices.

20. Abide in this pulsating experience of joyful radiance
for as long as you want. To finish, gather all the virtues
and lights back into the self-luminous inner jewel,
and completely rest your mind for a few breaths,
helping the healing energies to further integrate in
your body and energy system.

21. Then, activate the intention that your self-luminous
inner jewel will continue to shine from within,
keeping your body, energy, and mind balanced,

healthy, and clear, allowing you to become a beacon of harmony, creativity, joy, love, peace, and wisdom for all other sentient beings across all worlds.

HEALING BENEFITS

- Improving blood and energy circulation to the internal organs.
- Releasing toxins and emotions trapped in the internal organs and the tissues surrounding them.
- Rejuvenating our whole being by integrating our body, energy, and mind.
- Increasing our self-love and appreciation towards our life and our personal potential.
- Harmonizing our being with the sacred energies of the universal five elements.

PRACTICE INSIGHTS

The *Five Elements Healing Meditation* is a profoundly restorative and transformative practice that brings together all the healing meditation principles we have learned so far in this book. Building on all the previous principles, this practice introduces the healing lights, sounds, and virtues of the five elements.

Using the five elements lights and sounds harmonizes the fundamental energies that constitute our body and our environment. Bypassing the limitations of our intellect, which focuses on the material world, the sounds and colors of the five elements reawaken the natural healing intelligence of our body. This natural intelligence is the same natural intelligence that creates galaxies and keeps planets in orbit. When we allow this natural intelligence to do its job, it heals us and changes our experience of who we are in profound ways.

Awakening the virtues associated with each of the five elements further stimulates the profound changes initiated by the healing sounds and colors. By deliberately feeling love, joy, kindness, flexibility, stability, acceptance, perseverance, openness, good communication, and caring intimacy, we learn how to manifest at will these expressions of universal wisdom within us and allow them to guide us through our life journey.

To harmonize each level of organ function, we practice the healing sounds at three different volume levels: out loud, to address our physical body; whispered, to address our energetic system; and, silent-internal, to address our mind. Regardless of the volume we use, it is important to feel the healing sound vibrating in the actual organs and areas we are addressing. Feeling the vibration in the actual organ we intend to heal generates subtle tissue healing, allowing the organ to release stagnant toxicity, tension, and trauma. The directions for the practice tell us to rest our hands over each organ as we exhale while making the different healing sounds. Another option to further stimulate the organs is to massage or tap the area softly with our fists as we exhale.

Once we have harmonized each of the elements, we gather their colors and virtues to create our self-luminous inner jewel behind the navel. Besides grounding the empowered five elements behind the navel, our main energetic center, we can use the self-luminous inner jewel as an internal meditation support. Resting our attention on our inner jewel stabilizes our practice and helps awaken profound states of inner silence and mental clarity. Abiding in our inner jewel as the union of the virtues of the five elements can lead us to the experience of being beyond a sense of dualistic separation—me versus the world—from where many health issues originate.

The *Five Elements Healing Meditation* is a delightful gift that you can offer to yourself. As a gateway into the world of inner alchemy, the *Five Elements Healing Meditation* practice invites you to love yourself and achieve your temporary goals and dreams while guiding you towards your higher purposes in life. If you take the time to harmonize your inner five elements, their quintessential wisdom will assist you in healing your body, awakening your mind, and harmonizing your environment.

IV

HEALING WITH SELF-MASSAGE

THE DRY BATH SELF-MASSAGE

The *Dry Bath*, also known as the *Sitting Eight Brocades*, is a self-massage routine designed to keep our bodies young and healthy. This self-massage is called the *Dry Bath* because by softly brushing the surface of our physical body we "wash" our inner body, smoothing, stimulating, and increasing the flow of vital force through all our energetic channels. Because of its profound effect on the circulation of our vital force, the *Dry Bath* harmonizes our body, our energy, and our mind, creating the internal and external environment for healing and positive conditions to manifest in our life with ease.

The *Dry Bath* helps us heal and stay healthy because it invites the warmth of our loving touch to permeate to the core of every cell in our body. Through the comforting warmth of self-love, the *Dry Bath* self-massage benefits our internal organs and bodily functions, raising our vitality, improving our immunity, facilitating our digestion, and promoting our overall well-being.

Practicing the *Dry Bath* is an expression of love and gratitude to our physical form and, therefore, to ourselves. Besides its formidable benefits in repairing and maintaining the health of our physical body, the *Dry Bath* also helps us cultivate joyful emotions and awaken our mind by combining positive intention and sustained attention.

As with all other healing meditation practices, the *Dry Bath* is rooted in the understanding that the content of our mind determines the quality of our life. Obvious repetitive thought patterns, as well as more subtle layers of data stored and concealed within our subconscious awareness, imperceptibly dictate our life experience. When activated by circumstances, stored conscious and unconscious mental impressions function like pebbles thrown into a calm pond: they initiate and sustain ripples of energetic vibrations that resonate across our whole being, from our mind to our energetic system and then to our physical body.

To help us direct the inner processes that affect how we feel, the *Dry Bath* self-massage encourages us to deliberately focus on feelings of love, well-being, optimism, and abundance. When in the here and now we welcome life into our lives, life feels welcomed and blossoms, revealing its magical beauty.

Rubbing our hands and then gently brushing our skin with loving intention awakens our healing potential from within the command center inside each of our cells. When the trillions of cells that make up our body vibrate in joy, they transmit their joy into all aspects of our life.

Through the natural law of resonance and sympathetic vibration, when we appreciate ourselves, the universe responds accordingly and our body attracts more healing energy from our environment. To help us cultivate healing self-love, renew our view of life, and break free from giving our power away to old habits and pre-programmed mental patterns, the *Dry Bath* offers a simple a three-step process:

1. Choosing which positive energetic vibrations and feelings we want to embody and experience—with emphasis on joy and well-being.
2. Awakening within our body and mind those feelings of joy, well-being, and all other qualities we want to embody and experience.
3. Anchoring and reinforcing the positive energetic vibrations in our body and our mind through the light touch of gentle brushing.

Using this three-step process, we plant new seeds in our

body and mind and fertilize them with the love of our sustained attention. By sustaining a nurturing intention, we broadcast across our whole being that we are embracing and enjoying our greater potential. Through our regular practice of the *Dry Bath*, we gradually transform inner obstacles into the unwavering recognition that joy and well-being are the essence of who we are.

Happy, calm, and at ease with ourselves—and within ourselves—the *Dry Bath* guides us to recognize our vibrant physical body as a guesthouse for our spirit and to recognize our spirit as the offspring of the divine nature of the universe. In this state of graceful well-being and profound peace, we heal and thrive by enlivening the joyful experience of our universality.

ENERGETIC ANATOMY AND VITAL FORCE

Ancient healing traditions and modern science tell us that we live in a universe created, sustained, and recycled by universal energy. As the language of life itself, universal energy is the substance and the force that gives birth to and empowers everything we experience and perceive. From universal energy everything emanates, in it everything exists, and to it everything returns.

As the inner and outer ground of all that is, universal energy pervades everything and everywhere, creating a continuity of existence from denser material worlds to more subtle and spiritual realities. Providing a common basis of being, universal energy unites all things among themselves and with the universe itself. Even the space between objects, apparently empty to our ordinary senses, is a continuum of subtle universal energy.

In the context of healing meditation practice, we refer to this universal energy as "vital force." Being aware of the presence and flow of vital force in our life—even being open to the possibility of the existence of vital force—expands our experience of reality, playing an essential role in our healing and well-being. As Taoist physician master Hua Ching Ni explains:

> Vital force is the ultimate essence of the universe as well as the law of all movement. When it conglomerates, vital force is called matter. When it animates form, it is called life. When it separates and withdraws from form, it is called death. When vital force flows, there is health. When vital force is blocked, there is sickness and disease.

Since each of us is a microcosm of the universe, each of us is also a system of energies in motion that flows and vibrates in an ocean of vital force—the universe itself. Through different frequencies of vibration, our individual consciousness uses this universal energy to manifest in the physical plane as our human body, our network of energetic channels, and our mental functions.

The process of transforming universal energy into what we perceive as our physical body starts right at conception in our mother's womb. At the moment when the egg of our mother and the sperm from our father unite into one single cell, our consciousness is directed towards this first cell that is us. This original cell immediately starts replicating to become our fully developed physical body, around 400 trillion cells later.

What we see taking place on the physical level—a baby growing in the tummy of her mother—is supported by a subtle process where raw universal energy organizes itself into a system of individual energetic meridians. These meridians carry vital force to develop and nourish the different parts our individual body.

Once our body has fully formed and we are ready to be born, the network of energetic channels that processes universal energy into personal energy remains as the subtle expression of our nervous system, working along with the circulatory system of veins, arteries, and lymphatic vessels to promote the movement of bodily fluids and vital force in our body.

As long as our vital force flows smoothly through the network of energy channels (Fig. 4.1), we feel well, our mind is calm and clear, and we experience the joy and vastness of being alive. On the other hand, when due to developmental challenges, physical injuries, infections, emotional stress and trauma, detrimental lifestyle, and the influence of weather, our energetic channels are unbalanced, blocked, or drained, and acute symptoms of illness appear. If these symptoms are not remedied, chronic illness will manifest.

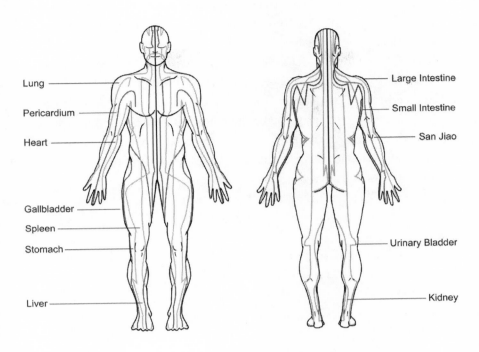

Figure 4.1
Acupuncture meridians chart.

The *Dry Bath* self-massage is an efficient method to help prevent and remedy imbalances in the energetic network of our body because it coordinates breathing, movement, touch, intention, and attention. The gentle brushing reestablishes the normal flow of vital force along the channels and redeploys back into the channels and inner organs any vital force that might have spread to the outer layers of our vibrational field. Once back in proper circulation, this recovered vital force is again available for the metabolic processes needed to maintain a healthy body. Because it helps us restore and maintain our body's natural flow of vital force, the *Dry Bath* gradually allows us to experience our personal energy field as an extension of the universal energy field, aligning our present situation with our divine potential.

The interrelation between our energetic system and our physical body continues from our conception until the time of our death, when our consciousness separates once and for all from our physical body. Before death, our consciousness also separates from our physical body during sleep. The difference between death and sleep is that at death our consciousness doesn't reenter our physical body. Instead, our physical body and our personal vital force gradually return to their respective sources and our consciousness continues its journey through different states of being that for a while are non-physical.

GENERAL PRACTICE CONSIDERATIONS

To maximize the benefits of the *Dry Bath*, consider the following suggestions as you practice:

- The main instruction is to gently brush your body. Simply relax, breathe, and brush yourself following the instructions of the sequence you will learn in the following section.
- As you lovingly brush, imagine that your body shines from within with white-golden light. Imagine the white-golden healing light spreading through the surface of your body and around you, dissolving tensions, blockages, and accumulated energetic debris.
- Keep in mind the key points from previous chapters: Breathe naturally, remain mindful, feel joyful, and smile to whatever parts you are brushing. Be playful, keep a light and positive attitude towards whatever comes to your mind.
- Maintain a loving awareness towards your body, regardless of things about your body you might dislike. Your loving awareness strengthens the self-massage effects by awakening the qualities and virtues associated with each organ system and energy channel as explained earlier in the *Five Elements Healing Meditation*.
- You can practice directly on your skin or over light clothing. Use your bare, dry hands. Do not apply any oil. Once you have started practicing, it is better not to add or remove any clothing until you have completed the sequence.
- Except where otherwise indicated, keep your tongue

lightly touching your upper palate throughout the practice.

- It is best to practice all the parts of the *Dry Bath* self-massage sequence in order. If you are pressed for time, or if you are addressing a specific health situation, you can do just the parts you believe will be most beneficial. However, the ideal situation is to develop the habit of doing the whole *Dry Bath* sequence once daily.

- The number of repetitions is flexible and depends on the amount of time you have for practice and what benefits you are trying to accomplish. For daily maintenance, ten repetitions of each part of the sequence are ideal, unless otherwise indicated in the directions. A shorter version, ideal to practice right before bed, is to do three repetitions of each part of the sequence. If you have time, you can do more repetitions. Also, it is ideal to dedicate more time to sensitive, tense, or painful areas.

- For regular practice and maintenance, the best practice times are upon waking up, before bedtime, and before and after meditation practice.

- To recover from illness or in the case of serious degenerative diseases, you can practice as many times a day as you wish. In these situations, you can practice lying down in bed or sitting on a reclining chair if necessary and do what you can while remaining comfortable. If you are too weak to move physically, you can imagine that you are practicing the *Dry Bath* and coordinate the breath with your inner visualization.

- Try to practice in a clean space with fresh air. Also, feel free to experiment practicing in nature and see if you notice any differences in how you feel afterwards.

- And, above all, enjoy yourself. It's all for fun!

THE DRY BATH
HEALING SELF-MASSAGE SEQUENCE

For a full video of the *Dry Bath Healing Self-Massage* go to:
www.joyfulheartinstitute.com/healing-now

1. Preparatory breathing:

The preparatory breathing steps are optional but highly recommended. They tell our body and mind that we are ready to feel well and stay well. The preparatory breathing steps are especially recommended when we practice self-massage before bedtime. At bedtime, they help us transition between the busy rhythm of our daily activity and the calmer and softer *Dry Bath* practice that will carry us into our sleep and dream states.

Part 1:

- Inhale through your nose, letting your shoulders lightly rise. (Fig. 4.2)
- Exhale through your mouth, making a gentle "Aaaahhh" sound. As you exhale, let your shoulders go back to a relaxed position and release all tension from your body and mind. (Fig. 4.3)
- Repeat this cycle three times.

Part 2:

- Breathe in and out through your nose, letting your breath naturally become slower.
- As you inhale, bring the tip of your tongue to touch

your upper palate, just behind the upper teeth.
- Hold your breath in for a brief moment, with the tongue still touching the upper palate.
- As you exhale, let your tongue rest down.
- Repeat this cycle nine times.

Figure 4.2
Inhale raising your shoulders.

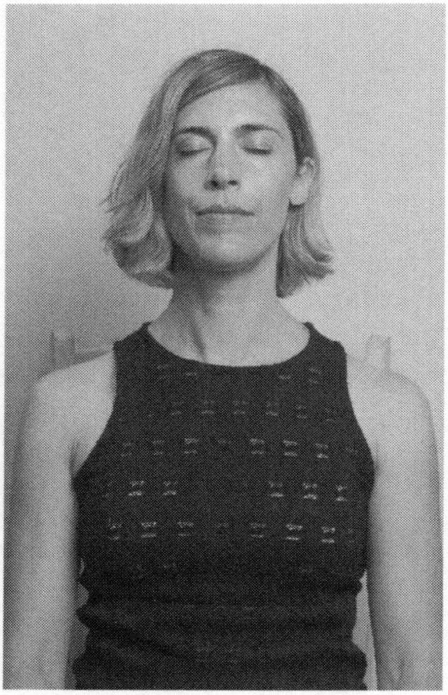

Figure 4.3
Exhale relaxing your shoulders.

2. Rubbing and washing the hands:

Rubbing our hands together at a slow and gentle pace stimulates the flow of energy and blood throughout our whole body. There are six energy channels in each arm, and because the energy in these channels is more accessible in the fingers, palms, and wrists, we can easily stimulate and balance the flow of vital force throughout our whole body by rubbing our hands. Because our vital force is in charge of moving the blood in our body, when we rub our hands and stimulate our vital force we are also stimulating and balancing the blood flow in our body.

176

Our body has two main groups of energy channels: one group is connected to our hands and the other group is connected to our feet. Because all the energy channels connected to our hands have a paired channel that connects to our feet, when we rub our hands we activate all the main energy meridians of the body. The table below shows the correspondence between the paired arm and leg energetic channels:

Arm Channels	Leg Channels
Lungs	Large Intestine
Kidneys	Bladder
Liver	Gallbladder
Heart	Small Intestine
Pancreas – Spleen	Stomach
Pericardium	San Jiao

DIRECTIONS

- Rub your palms until they feel warm. Imagine the warmth as golden light that expands from your palms, filling up and surrounding your arms, chest, abdomen, and legs. (Fig. 4.4)
- Rest your left palm on your left knee. With your right palm brush back and forth ten times the top of your left hand. (Fig. 4.5)
- Repeat on the right side.

3. *Washing the arms:*

Each arm has six energy channels: the lung, pericardium, and heart channels are in the inner side of our arm. (Fig. 4.6) The large intestine, san jiao, and small intestine channels are in the outer side of our arm. (Fig. 4.7)

Figure 4.4
Rubbing the hands.

Figure 4.5
Brushing the top of the hand.

When our vital force flows along these channels smoothly, our body has an easier time staying healthy and strong. When these channels have blockages, our vital force slows down and our body weakens.

Brushing our arms is especially beneficial to strengthen our respiratory function and supports our lungs as they experience the effects of conditions such as allergies, asthma, obstructive pulmonary disease, and emphysema. Brushing our arms also helps increase our overall energy and immunity, being especially indicated for people who are frequently ill.

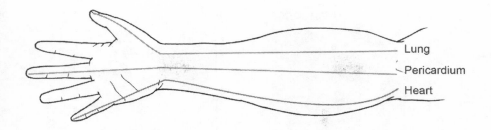

Figure 4.6.
Energetic channels inner arm.

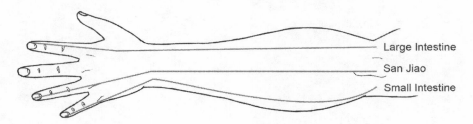

Figure 4.7
Energetic channels outer arm.

DIRECTIONS

- Rub your palms until they feel warm.
- Using your right palm, brush your left inner arm, ascending from the tip of your left hand to your left upper chest and inner shoulder. (Fig. 4.8)
- Turn your left palm to face down.
- Go around your shoulder and descend brushing the outer side of your arm to the tip of your left hand. (Fig. 4.9)
- Repeat brushing your left arm three to ten times.
- Repeat the whole sequence on your right arm, starting with rubbing your palms.

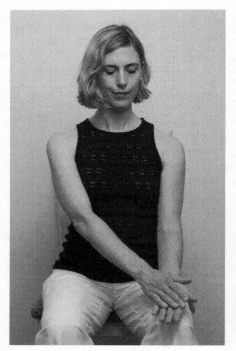

Figure 4.8
Brushing the inner arm up.

Figure 4.9
Brushing the outer arm down.

4. Washing the head:

All the energy channels of our body connect—directly or indirectly—to our head. Therefore, brushing our head has a beneficial effect on our whole being, helping us have a healthy and youthful appearance.

Brushing our head and scalp stimulates and balances the flow of vital force and blood to our face and our brain. Harmonizing the flow of vital force and blood in our brain has a positive effect on our nervous system, helping us reduce stress, prevent headaches, and improve our overall mental function.

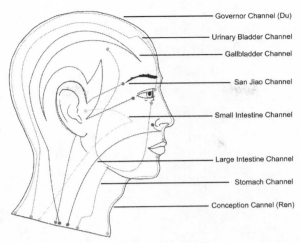

Figure 4.10
Acupuncture channels on the head.

In addition, when we brush our head, we also benefit our sense organs—ears, eyes, tongue, mouth, and nose. Because each of our sense organs has direct connections with specific internal organs and bodily functions, brushing and massaging them benefits both the sense organs and the inner organs and bodily functions connected with them. In the following table you can see the basic connections and correspondences between our sense organs and their related internal organs, tissues, and functions:

Sense Organ	Related Inner Organs	Related Tissues	Related Functions
Nose	Lung and Large Intestine	Skin, hair, throat	Smelling, breathing, immunity
Ears	Kidneys and Urinary Bladder	Bones, teeth, brain	Hearing, reproduction, long term memory
Eyes	Liver and Gallbladder	Tendons, nails, genitalia	Vision, planning, emotional balance
Mouth	Pancreas and Stomach	Four limbs, gums, breasts	Digestion, reasoning, concentration
Tongue	Heart and Small Intestine	Blood vessels, vocal cords	Taste, calmness, short term memory

181

To brush our face, we use the palms of our hands. To brush our scalp and the back of our head, we use the tips of our fingers. In both cases we apply light pressure.

Figure 4.11
Brushing face and head
from front to back.

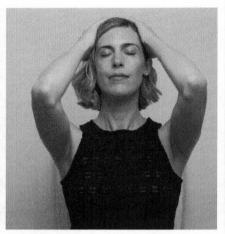

Figure 4.12
Brushing face and head
from back to front.

Figure 4.13
Brushing below the eyes.
Start at the nose.

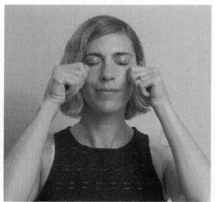

Figure 4.14
Brushing below the eyes.
Move towards the temples.

- Rub your palms until they feel warm.
- Using the palms of your hands, brush upwards, starting from your chin to the crown of your head. Continue down the back of the head to your neck. (Fig. 4.11)
- Repeat the brushing three to ten times.
- Reverse the direction of brushing. Starting at the back of your neck, go up to your crown and down the face to your chin. (Fig. 4.12)
- Repeat the brushing three to ten times.

5. Washing the eyes and temples:

Brushing our eyes and the structures around them benefits our vision. We have two types of vision: *External vision* allows us to see the world around us. *Internal vision* allows us to connect with our intuition and creativity. *Internal vision* also allows us to see our essence and the essence of the world around us beyond physical appearances. When our internal and external visions are in harmony, we feel at ease in the world and we can clearly see what we want our life to look like and how to accomplish it.

Our eyes, though, are often tired from staring at the computer and other screens. Overusing our eyes once they are already tired, especially when we use technology after sunset, diminishes our inner vision. When our inner vision diminishes, we feel blind to our inner nature, becoming easily stressed, anxious, and fearful.

Overusing our eyes also has an overall negative effect on our health because of their energetic connection with our liver, which is the main toxicity filter and hormonal regulator in our body.

The energetic meridians of the stomach, large intestine, bladder, and gallbladder also connect to the eyes. For this reason, brushing our eyes has a positive effect on our overall well-being.

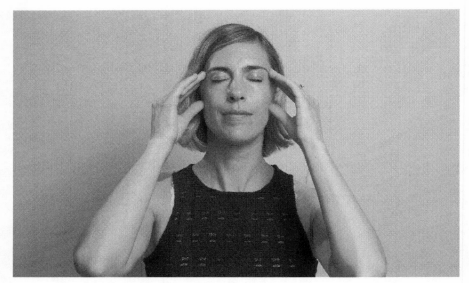

Figure 4.15
Brushing the temples.

Part 1:

- Rub your palms until they feel warm.
- Place your palms on your face, covering your eyes.
- As you breathe in, absorb the warmth from your palms into your eyes. As you breathe out, feel your eyes and face muscles releasing tension and feeling rejuvenated.
- Repeat the above three steps three to ten times.

Part 2:

- Rub your thumbs until they feel warm.
- Holding the tip of your thumb with your index finger, brush the ridge of your eye sockets, from your nose to your temples, first above and then below the eye. (Fig. 4.14 and 4.15)
- Repeat three to ten times.

Part 3:

- Place your thumbs below your cheekbones and your index, middle, and ring fingers on your temples. (Fig. 4.15)
- In a circular motion, brush your temples with your thumbs towards the back three to ten times.
- Reverse the direction and brush your temples with the thumbs towards the back three to ten times.

6. *Looking up, down, and to the sides*

Our eyes are sustained physically by a set of muscles and energetically by the channels that start and end there. When we purposely work these muscles and channels, we strengthen our eyes, improve our vision, and relieve eyestrain.

Gently stretching our eyes in the four directions also tones the glands and drainage ducts that keep our eyes moist. This stimulates the production of tears, helps relieve eye dryness, and keep our eyes cleaner by flushing debris from their surface. As you practice, move your eyes slowly, without causing strain or discomfort.

DIRECTIONS

- Look straight ahead with your eyes open.
- Beginning with your eyes up, look up and down three times.
- Beginning with your eyes down, look down and up three times.
- Beginning with your eyes towards the right, look right and left three times.
- Beginning with your eyes towards the left, look left and right three times.

7. *Washing the nose:*

Brushing our nose and pressing on its bridge energizes the outside and inside of our nose and sinuses, helping us breathe better and helping to prevent and resolve acute and chronic issues like nasal obstruction, inflammation, and infection. Keeping the energy around our nose vibrant strengthens our immune defense and helps us prevent becoming ill, since often colds and flus start with pathogens entering through our nostrils.

The energetic channels of our lungs, large intestine, stomach, and urinary bladder travel from our fingers and toes to our nose. For this reason, brushing our nose benefits not only our respiratory system, but also our digestive and elimination systems.

Since we receive the breath of life through our nose, besides benefiting our physical health, brushing our nose also helps us find mental and emotional balance. In this sense, our nose is like the gate of a sacred temple: it connects our inner being with the outer world. In addition, by keeping the energy in and around our nose vibrant, we also help our voice and shape how we express our inner desires to the outer world.

 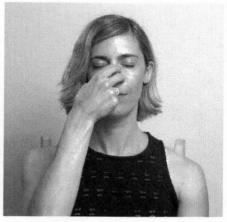

Figure 4.16
Washing the nose.

Figure 4.17
Pressing the bridge of the nose.

Part 1:

- Rub the index and middle fingers of both hands until they feel warm.
- Brush the sides of your nose up and down with the inner side of your index and middle fingers. (Fig. 4.16)
- Repeat ten times.

Part 2:

- Use the thumb, index and middle fingers of the right hand to gently press and release the nose bridge.
- Press as you inhale, release as you exhale. (Fig. 4.17)
- Repeat three to ten times with the right hand and then with the left hand.

8. Washing the ears and teeth:

Our ears and teeth are directly related to the kidney system, which is the foundation of our long-term well-being. As the sense organ related to the kidneys, rubbing our ears supports our hearing, strengthens our energetic resources, balances our nervous system and grounds us in the present moment. Also, as our hands and feet, our ears have hundreds of energy points that connect with the rest of our whole body. For this reason, massaging our ears benefits our overall health and well-being.

Softly biting our teeth and swishing saliva has a beneficial effect on our teeth and gums. Our teeth are energetically connected to our kidneys and to most of the energy channels of our digestive system. Clicking our teeth softly strengthens those systems and revitalizes our whole body.

Clicking our teeth softly also stimulates the salivary glands. Even though saliva is mostly water, it is essential for our well-being. Saliva contains electrolytes, antibacterial compounds, and various enzymes. Saliva protects teeth from decay, promotes proper digestion, supports general immunity, and reduces acidity in the body. Empowering saliva by clicking our teeth and then swallowing that saliva empowers the immunity or our digestive system, strengthens our bones, and increases our energy storage.

DIRECTIONS

Part 1:

- Rub your palms until they feel warm.
- Using your thumb and index finger, rub your ears from top to bottom.
- Repeat three times.

Part 2:

- Close your mouth naturally and gently bite 36 times. (Saliva might start accumulating in your mouth. Don't swallow it; it will be used for the next step.)

Part 3:

- Once you are done clicking your teeth, close your eyes and swish the saliva inside your mouth 36 times.
- After swishing, swallow the empowered saliva divided in three swallows, directing the movement towards your navel.

9. Washing the chest and abdomen up and down:

Our chest and abdomen hold our internal organs. When we brush these areas, we benefit all our inner organs, especially our lungs, heart, stomach, large intestine, liver, and pancreas. Supporting the function of these organs has a beneficial effect in our overall well-being.

Washing our chest and abdomen especially promotes better digestion and immunity. It is also a relaxing movement that promotes self-love.

For women, washing the chest and abdomen stimulates the energetic and lymphatic flow in the breasts.

DIRECTIONS

- Rub your palms until they feel warm.
- Place your palms on your inner hips. (Fig. 4.18)
- Brush straight up to the upper chest (Fig. 4.19) and then back down to the hips.
- Repeat three to ten times.

Figure 4.18
Brushing up and down
starting position.

Figure 4.19
Brushing up and down
upper position.

10. Washing the chest and abdomen diagonally:

Washing the chest and abdomen diagonally shares the same principles as the previous part of the self-massage sequence. But now we use only one hand at a time with diagonal movement, instead of both hands straight up and down.

As explained earlier, washing our chest and abdomen benefits all our inner organs, in this case especially our heart, digestive, and elimination systems. Washing our chest and abdomen also promotes better immunity. In addition, for women, it contributes to balance the hormonal and reproductive systems.

Figure 4.20
Brushing diagonally
starting position.

Figure 4.21
Brushing diagonally
upper position.

- Rub your palms until they feel warm.
- Place your left palm over the left hip. (Fig. 4.20)
- Brush upwards, diagonally towards the right shoulder (Fig. 4.21) and back down to the left hip.
- Repeat the brushing three to ten times.
- Repeat the whole sequence with your right palm from the right side, starting with rubbing your palms.

11. Washing the diaphragm:

Our diaphragm is a thin muscle that separates our abdomen from our chest. It is located just below our lungs and heart, on top of our liver, stomach, and pancreas. Due to stress and poor posture, our diaphragm easily gets tense, affecting our digestion, breathing, and our overall health. Brushing our diaphragm has a beneficial effect on our respiration, digestive, and elimination systems.

DIRECTIONS

- Rub your palms until they feel warm.
- Place your left palm over your liver, on the right side of your ribcage, and your right palm behind your pancreas, on the left side of your ribcage, around the back. (Fig. 4.22)
- Brush both palms across the diaphragm, in opposite directions.
- When you reach the other side, switch hand positions and brush again. (Fig. 4.23)
- Repeat three to ten times.

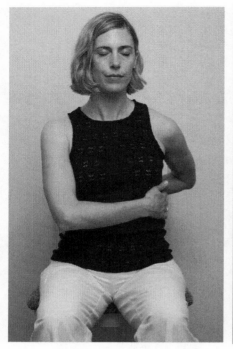

Figure 4.22
Brushing diaphragm.
Starting position.

Figure 4.23
Brushing diaphragm.
Switching hands position.

12. Washing the abdomen:

Our abdomen is the root of our physical vitality and mental stability. From our navel we were connected to our mother as we developed in her womb. After birth, the navel still remains the most important energetic center to support our vitality.

Washing our abdomen increases our vitality and stimulates the flow of energy through our whole body. It specifically benefits the large and small intestines, promoting better digestion, absorption of nutrients, and elimination of waste. In addition, washing our abdomen is a centering practice that provides clarity of purpose in life.

- Rub your palms until they feel warm.
- Place your right hand on the right side of your waist, with the thumb in the front and the other fingers in the back. (Fig. 4.24)
- Place the palm of your left hand on your solar plexus.
- Circle ten times counter-clockwise, starting at the solar plexus, down to the pubic bone, and back to the solar plexus.
- Switch hands and circle ten times clockwise.
- Once you are done with both directions, place your palms on top of your navel and take three deep, slow breaths.

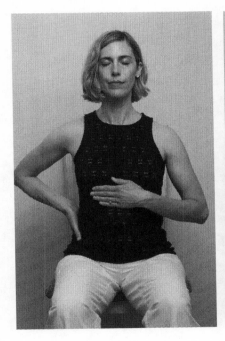 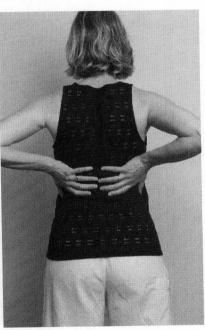

Figure 4.24
Brushing the abdomen.

Figure 4.25
Brushing kidneys.

13. Washing the kidneys:

Along with our liver, our kidneys are essential to our well-being because they are in charge of eliminating toxic substances from our body. Brushing and warming up the lumbar area strengthens both our kidney function and our lower back.

Besides its direct effect on filtration and elimination, brushing our kidneys can also benefit cases of high blood pressure, insomnia, and respiratory issues. Brushing our kidneys also complements and strengthens the benefits of brushing our abdomen. Mentally, nourishing our kidneys gives us persistence to act based on the clarity we enlivened by brushing our abdomen.

DIRECTIONS

- Rub your palms until they feel warm.
- Place your palms over your low back. (Fig. 4.25)
- Inhale and, holding your breath, apply moderate pressure as you rub up and down your low back.
- Once you feel the need to exhale, let the air go out. Inhale again, hold the air and repeat the up and down brushing.
- Repeat for three breaths.
- Try to build up holding your breath until you can massage up and down 36 times in one breath.
- Once you are done, place your palms on top of your navel and take three slow, deep breaths.

If holding the breath is uncomfortable, simply rub your lower back up and down.

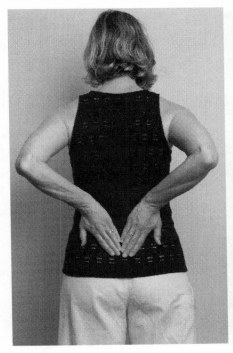
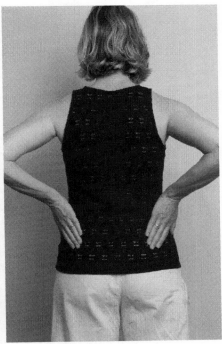

Figure 4.26
Brushing the sacrum.
Starting position.

Figure 4.27
Brushing Sacrum.
Reaching the outer waist.

14. Washing the sacrum, waist and upper buttocks:

Brushing our sacrum, waist, and upper buttocks improves overall blood circulation, releases body tension, and improves nervous system function. Because our sacrum is the end of our spine, its state directly influences our brain and the nerves that run down our legs to our toes. Therefore, brushing our sacrum and waist is also beneficial to relieve pain due to sciatica and neuropathies.

Our waist connects our upper and lower bodies. From too much sitting, this area gets tense, which reduces blood circulation and causes back pain and congestion in the reproductive organs. Brushing our waist and upper buttocks has a beneficial effect on our lower back and improves the function of our reproductive system.

- Rub your palms until they feel warm.
- Place the tips of both hands on the upper sacrum. (Fig. 4.26)
- Applying moderate pressure, rub down to the tailbone and back up, ten times.
- Keeping the same up-and-down motion, start massaging along your waistline to the side of your body and then back to your sacrum. (Fig. 4.27)

15. Washing the legs:

Brushing our legs strengthens our digestive and urinary functions, increasing overall energy and relieving fatigue. It also helps relieve hemorrhoids, prolapsed organs, poor balance, and weak gait.

Each leg has six energy channels: our spleen, kidney, and liver channels run up from the tips of the toes to the abdomen and chest along the inside of the legs; our stomach, urinary bladder, and gallbladder channels run down from our head to the tips of our toes along the outside of the leg. By maintaining the open flow of these channels, our body has an easier time remaining healthy and strong. When these channels have blockages, vital force slows down and our body weakens. Brushing our legs helps keep those energy channels free of obstructions.

- Rub your palms until they feel warm.
- Place one palm on each side of your upper left thigh. (Fig. 4.28)
- Brush both sides of your leg down to your ankle. (Fig. 4.29) At your ankle, move your palms to the back of your leg and brush up the back of the leg to your upper thigh.
- Repeat the brushing three to ten times.

- Repeat the whole sequence on your right side, starting with rubbing your palms.

Figure 4.28
Brushing the leg downward.

Figure 4.29
Brushing the leg upward.

16. Washing the knees:

Our knees have a direct relationship with our kidneys and lower back. Therefore, in addition to benefitting our knees, rubbing our knees helps strengthen and relax our lower back, helping our spine and muscles. Brushing our knees stimulates the flow of vital force and blood in our legs and knees. Brushing our knees also has a beneficial effect on our sexual and reproductive functions.

Mentally, our knees have an influence on the strength of our willpower. Brushing our knees strengthens our determination and helps us stay firm in what we believe is right regardless of external difficulties and challenges.

Part 1:
- Rub your palms until they feel warm.
- Place one palm on each side of your left knee. (Fig. 4.30)
- Applying moderate pressure, rub your knee down, behind (Fig. 4.31) and up again.
- Repeat the brushing three to ten times.
- Repeat the whole sequence on your right knee, starting with rubbing your palms.

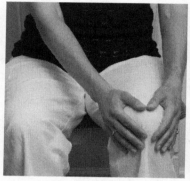

Figure 4.30
Brushing knee. Starting position.

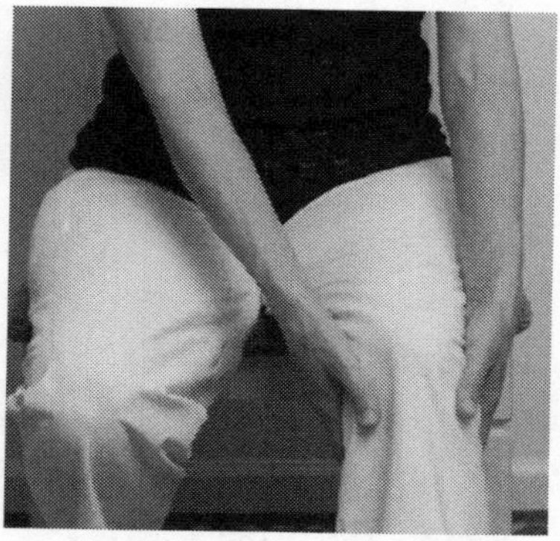

Figure 4.31
Brushing knee. Back position.

Part 2:
- Rub your palms until they feel warm.
- Place one palm on each knee. (Fig. 4.32)
- Applying moderate pressure, rub your knees in a circular motion, first one direction and then the reverse. (Fig. 4.33)
- Repeat the rubbing three to ten times in each direction.

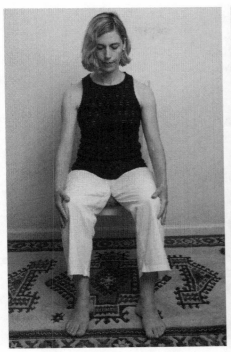
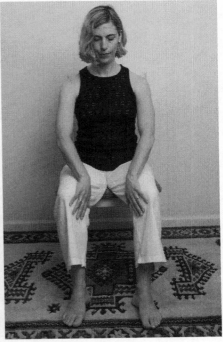

Figure 4.32
Brushing knees outwards.

Figure 4.33
Brushing knees inwards.

17. *Washing the feet:*

Our feet have thousands of nerve endings that connect with every part of our body. (Fig. 4.34) Rubbing and pressing these energetic points strengthens the health of our whole body. It also helps us remain grounded and present, increasing self-affection, and the will to walk our life path with joy and determination.

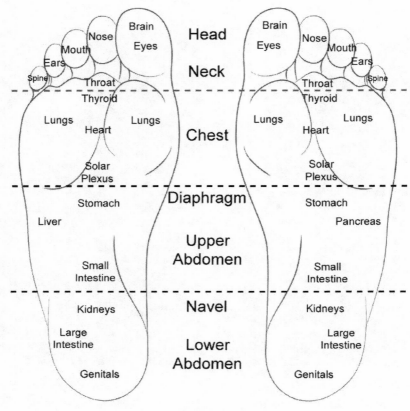

Figure 4.34
Feet areas related to other body parts.

DIRECTIONS

Part 1:

- Hold your left foot with both hands.
- Imagine three lines on the sole of the foot: from your little toe to the outer side of the heel; from your middle toes to the center of the heel; and from your big toe to the inner side of your heel. (Fig. 4.35)
- Using your thumbs, press the sole of your left foot

along those lines, starting from the little toe and
finishing on the inner side of the heel.
- Repeat the whole sequence on the right sole.

Part 2:
- Rub your palms until they feel warm.
- With your left hand, hold the toes of your left foot
  from above, pulling them slightly backwards. (Fig.
  4.36)
- With you right hand, brush the arch of your left foot
  ten times.
- Repeat the whole sequence on the right side, starting
  with rubbing your palms.

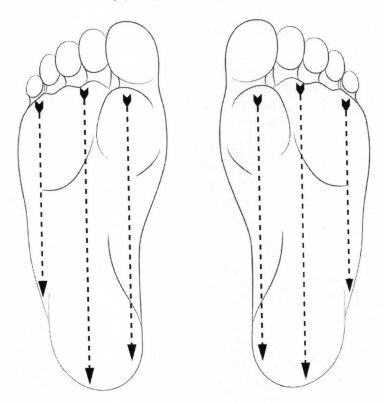

Figure 4.35
Lines for massaging the sole of your feet.

18. Brushing the lower abdomen:

The lower abdomen holds our main personal energetic savings account. Through brushing our lower abdomen we increase the "funds" in that account, replenishing energetically our body. Brushing our lower abdomen grounds us, provides us with a feeling of centeredness, and nourishes our whole being.

Because it promotes nutrient and mineral absorption, softly brushing the lower abdomen strengthens our deepest resources. Brushing our lower abdomen also recharges our hormonal and reproductive systems, regulating and increasing sexual and reproductive energy.

DIRECTIONS

This is the only part of the self-massage sequence where the practice is slightly different for women and men.

For women:
-   Rub your palms until they feel warm.
-   Place your left hand on your waist and your right palm just below your navel. (Fig. 4.37)
-   Circle your right hand ten times counter-clockwise, starting just below the navel down to the pubic bone and back to the navel.
-   Switch hands and circle another ten times clockwise.

For men:
-   Rub your palms until they feel warm.
-   With your left hand, cup your testicles. Place your right palm just below your navel.
-   Circle your right hand ten times counter-clockwise, starting just below the navel down to the pubic bone and back to the navel.
-   Switch hands and circle another ten times clockwise.

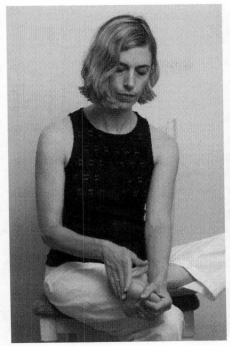
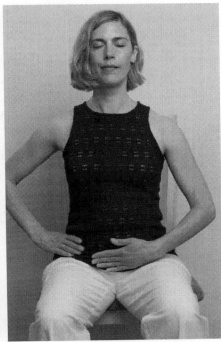

Figure 4.36
Brushing foot.

Figure 4.37
Brushing lower abdomen.
(Female position.)

For those suffering or recovering from chronic illnesses, especially serious degenerative diseases, it is highly beneficial to increase the number of *Brushing the lower abdomen* repetitions to 81 for each side. In healing meditation, it is considered that 81 repetitions activate the whole range of healing energies within our energy system.

19. Concluding meditation:

After completing the whole self-massage sequence, take a few minutes to let your body integrate and enjoy the renewed flow of vital force. You can do this sitting or lying down.

- Feel how your body is vibrant, relaxed, and soft. Let go of any remaining tension. You are complete. There is nothing else to do.
- Simply rest at peace in openness, enjoying the moment. Bask in the renewed warmth of well-being, love, and joy.
- Rest like this for five minutes. Then move on to the next step in your practice or go back to your day, bringing to the world your wonderful joy of being.
- If you practiced the self-massage right before bed, you can simply lie down to sleep, maintaining a soft sense of blissful awareness.

THE DRY BATH
HEALING SELF-MASSAGE SEQUENCE
EXERCISE LIST

The following list with the elements of the *Dry Bath* self-massage can be useful to remind you of the sequence as you practice:

1. *Preparatory breathing*
2. *Rubbing and washing the hands*
3. *Washing the arms*
4. *Washing the head*
5. *Washing the eyes and temples*
6. *Looking up, down, and to the sides*
7. *Washing the nose*
8. *Washing the ears and teeth*
9. *Washing the chest and abdomen up and down*
10. *Washing the chest and abdomen diagonally*
11. *Washing the diaphragm*
12. *Washing the abdomen*
13. *Washing the kidneys*
14. *Washing the sacrum, waist, and upper buttocks*
15. *Washing the legs*
16. *Washing the knees*
17. *Washing the feet*
18. *Brushing the lower abdomen*
19. *Concluding meditation*

V

THE TREASURE OF THE WISE

"Constantly remember this:
Being kind and having a good heart
Are the essential meditation instructions.

Love, compassion and the wish that all beings—
Without exception—attain the bliss of complete awakening
Are the root of our well-being and spiritual path."

~Patrul Rinpoche

CONTINUING OUR JOURNEY

"Life is indeed a state of mind."
~Chime Dorje

Congratulations, we have reached the end of *Healing Now*. The essence of our journey has been to experience well-being by cultivating a loving heart and a wakeful mind. Now, it is important to continue with our daily practice, integrating what we have learned and practiced during these previous weeks together.

One way to integrate everything learned is to maintain a morning and evening practice. In the morning, while still lying down in bed, as soon as we realize we are awake, we can practice the *Healing Smile*. This will take just a couple of minutes and it will help us start our day with a sense of well-being, direction, and optimism. Then, before breakfast, we can have a meditation session that includes:

- Our personal and altruistic motivations.
- Centering and Purifying Breathing.
- A few minutes of The Sound of the Breath, The Three Alignments, Resting In the Narrow Gates, or any other of the healing mediation practices based on what we need to support us in our day.
- Dedication of our practice.

In the evening, before bed, we can have a meditation session that includes:

- Our personal and altruistic motivation.
- Centering and Purifying Breathing.
- The Dry Bath Self-Massage.
- Five Elements Healing Meditation.
- Dedication of our practice.

This is an example of how we can use the material that we have learned in *Healing Now* in three daily short practices that will take about 30 minutes of our day. However, as long as we maintain the main structure of practice, starting with our motivation and ending with our dedication, we can create a personal plan that addresses our own life circumstances.

What is essential is to maintain a daily practice. Our regularity and persistence help us to cultivate a steady, mindful, loving awareness that gradually pervades all moments and situations. Through the expansion of our loving heart and wakeful mind, we can continue to experience finer states of well-being and to mature our appreciation for the single, vibrant, and self-aware nature that pervades and connects all life—the essence of life itself.

Certain about the vastness and simplicity of our being, we connect with all that is in a profound way beyond boundaries of any kind. Abiding in this certainty, we understand how to heal and, at the same time, we understand that there is nothing to be healed because our nature—the essence of all things—is beyond health and illness, beyond gain and loss, beyond birth and death.

As this profound realization changes our view and experience of our world, our world changes with us. Aware that—while in the world and from the world—our essence is beyond worldly constraints, our obsession with finding pleasure and avoiding discomfort turns into openness towards how the present moment manifests. This rejuvenating openness allows us to further enjoy our physical form and our world as they are, while still attempting to transform them into what we would like them to be. In this regard, healing meditation provides us with a framework to recognize that life is a dream, so we can relax, and also to make it a fun and worthwhile dream, so we can enjoy.

Our healing meditation practice is a precious gift we can offer to this world since it encourages us to silently share our inner happiness through our smile, joy, kindness, and wakeful presence, wherever we go and with whomever we encounter. Our healing meditation practice invites us to be part of an epidemic of joyful people that relate, support, and even challenge each other through open, loving, and clear communication.

The essence of it all is to live in a state of wakeful, loving, and joyful presence, whenever and wherever we are. This essence is the seed of all happiness, the treasure in the heart of the wise.

JOYFUL HEART HEALING MEDITATION AND SELF-DEVELOPMENT PROGRAM

"You are the light of the world."
~Matthew 5:14

The Joyful Heart Self-Development Program, offered through the Joyful Heart Institute, is a system of teachings and practices that guides us to experience well-being, to unfold our life purposes, and to connect with our spiritual nature. Caring for our personal goals as well as for the well-being of our family and our community, the Joyful Heart program integrates the essence of ancient healing and spiritual wisdom with life coaching and modern psychology and neuroscience. This blending of ancient and modern wisdom provides us with a clear path for personal growth that quickly develops results and promotes profound changes in our being.

Through a sequence of 12 modules of teachings and practices, the Joyful Heart Self-Development Program offers us tools to:

- Support our health and well-being.
- Balance our emotions and reconnect with positivity and optimism.
- Develop self-love and appreciation for ourselves.
- Define and unfold clear purposes, visions, and goals.
- Cultivate a calm, clear, loving, and playful mind to address stressful situations.
- Connect with our inner sources of abundance and creativity.
- Maintain harmonious and fulfilling relationships.
- Help our family promote healthy habits and overcome destructive patterns.
- Contribute to the positive evolution of life and consciousness in our community and our world.

Joyful Heart Self-Development Program Sequence of Modules:

Module 1 – "Healing Now: Self-Healing and Rejuvenation"
Module 2 – "The Joy of Meditation: Awakening Our Mind"
Module 3 – "Connecting With Our Inner Guide: Purpose, Vision, Goals"
Module 4 – "Purification and Transforming Our Emotions"
Module 5 – "Healing Mantras and Sacred Sound: Enhancing Our Lives Through the Power of Resonance"
Module 6 – "The Five Elements In Daily Life: Self-Care, Nutrition, and Inner Alchemy"
Module 7 – "Relationships and Sexual Alchemy: The Teachings of the Sun and the Moon"
Module 8 – "Rediscovering Our Family, Rediscovering Ourselves"
Module 9 – "Dream, Death, and Transcendence Practices"
Module 10 – "Sacred Geometry and Space Harmonization: The Art of the Ancient Master Builders"
Module 11 – "Pilgrimage and Energetic Journeys"
Module 12 – "Remembering the Light of Our Heart"

MODULE 1
"HEALING NOW: SELF-HEALING AND REJUVENATION"

The first step in the Joyful Heart program is to mindfully connect with our vital force in the present moment. This connection establishes the ground for our healing and spiritual journey. Once we connect with our vital force in the present moment, it is easier for us to heal our body, calm our mind, and unfold our goals in life for our benefit and the benefit of the world.

In this first module, we learn how our body, energy, and mind interact with each other. We also learn how to use their interaction to transform stress, worry, and fatigue, into joy, clarity, and well-being. To support this transformation, we use breathing exercises, revitalizing self-massage, rejuvenating gentle movement (Qi Gong and Dao-In yoga), the *Healing Smile*, and the *Five Elements Healing*

Meditation practice. These practices are intended to become part of our daily routine to help us regain and maintain our well-being and live a joyful life.

MODULE 2
"THE JOY OF MEDITATION: AWAKENING OUR MIND"

The Joy of Meditation module is the central vein of the Joyful Heart program. Building on the foundation established in the first module, this second module expands our practice from focusing on healing and well-being towards the maturation of our inner divine potential.

Based on the progression of five principles—Arriving, Relaxing, Focusing, Exploring, and Resting—the *Joy of Meditation* module provides us with a clear and simple structure to unfold the natural calmness, stability, and clarity of our mind. The five principles of *The Joy of Meditation* can also be applied to enhance all aspects of our life.

MODULE 3
"CONNECTING WITH OUR INNER GUIDE: PURPOSE, VISION, GOALS"

Building on the first two modules of the program, the third module guides us to establish a clear connection with our inner guide. Our inner guide is the voice and expression of the sacred presence within us, or our awakened, inner nature. This sacred wisdom is always with us, whispering to us suggestions to enjoy ourselves and make our lives meaningful; yet, to perceive our inner guide and to interpret its guidance with clarity, we often have to listen beyond our intellect, beyond our limited, temporary ego, and beyond the conventions of the material world.

Experiencing our inner guide with clarity is of the greatest significance because it helps us make decisions, it keeps us connected to the higher aspects of our life purpose, and it pervades our daily lives with a profound sense of playful sacredness. Experiencing our inner guide empowers us to embrace our potential for personal fulfillment and to support others to recognize their own playful sacredness.

MODULE 4
"PURIFICATION AND TRANSFORMING OUR EMOTIONS"

The fourth module has two sections: the first section explores the practices of purification. Purification is the process of allowing our potential of being to shine by removing subtle blockages from our energy channels and our mind. These subtle inner blockages, often held in place by repetitive mental patterns and limiting beliefs, may manifest as physical, emotional, and mental issues, either within our individual lives or within our family lives.

The purification practices open us to experience our innate, joyful, pure nature and bask in the virtues of our heart—love, compassion, joy, and equanimity—from where we can more deeply enjoy life's magic and be of benefit to all beings.

The second section of this module explores the transformation of emotions to help us maintain well-being, stabilize our connection with our inner guide, and increase the positive flow of energy in our life. Transforming emotions means realizing that they are the natural expression of energy movements within our being as we meet life's situations. Therefore, once our energy system is more in tune with our inner guide, we can use our emotions as part of our navigation system in life. To understand our emotional system, we explore the concept of the Six Basic Human Needs to help us learn where we are operating from and how to consciously make the necessary adjustments to develop emotional maturity.

MODULE 5
"HEALING MANTRAS AND SACRED SOUND:
ENHANCING OUR LIVES THROUGH THE POWER OF RESONANCE"

This module explores sound as a transformative force that can promote our well-being, awaken our minds, harmonize our surroundings, and connect us to the inner nature of life. Since ancient times, healing and spiritual traditions have known that we are vibrational beings living in a vibrational universe. The practitioners of these traditions realized that the vibration of sound is a powerful means for healing and spiritual evolution. The reason is that sound, combined with our breathing, has the unique ability to quickly integrate our body, our energy, and mind our mind.

Sacred sounds and healing mantras are sounds that create a deep level of integration within individuals, families, and communities, helping us restore inner balance, transform outer obstacles, create positive life circumstances, connect with our essential nature, and develop insight into the essence of life.

Using sacred sound and healing mantras is one of the simplest and most convenient spiritual practices we can engage in. This practice can be performed anytime and any place, both internally and externally. The regular repetition of sacred sounds and healing mantras is an easy practice that can provide truly wonderful results, creating deep transformation in us, without the time demands of other practices that require long retreats and sustained effort.

Some of the key topics of this module are: the divine origin of sound; the healing power of speech; how sound impacts our body and mind; how to improve prayer through the power of sacred sound; and mantras for healing, longevity, prosperity, happiness, compassion, and liberation.

Module 6
"The Five Elements In Daily Life:
Self-Care, Nutrition, and Inner Alchemy"

In this module, we learn how to apply the wisdom of the healing and spiritual practitioners from the past to our daily life. As we read in *The Yellow Emperor's Classic of Medicine*, the foundation text of Chinese medicine, compiled around 4,600 years ago: "In the past, people practiced the Tao, the Way of Life. They understood the principle of balance, as represented by the transformations of the five elements and the energies of the universe. They formulated exercises to promote energy flow to harmonize themselves with the universe. They ate a balanced diet at regular times, arose and retired at regular hours, avoided overstressing their bodies and minds, and refrained from overindulgence of all kinds. They maintained well-being of body and mind; thus, it is not surprising that they lived over one hundred years without showing signs of aging."

Based on observing nature's rhythms and relations, the ancient healing and spiritual practitioners understood that our bodies, as well as the world that surrounds us, are made from five basic building blocks. They called these "Elements" and named them according to nature's foundations: Water, Wood, Fire, Earth, and Metal. These practitioners realized that by following the cycle of these energies during the year and adjust to their changes, it is easier to keep our bodies in good health and thrive in life. The Wisdom of the Five Elements is a tremendous treasure to enrich our daily life and our understanding of the universe.

This module focuses on learning to observe and follow the natural rhythms to maintain well-being. From that observation, the module offers suggestions for our lives in regards to hygiene, nutrition, herbal support, exercise, immunity, sexuality, sleeping, and spiritual practice.

Module 7
"Relationships and Sexual Alchemy:
The Teachings of the Sun and the Moon"

This module is divided in two sections: Relationships and Sexuality. In the first section, we explore the energetics of relationships, with emphasis on how we relate to ourselves—the foundation of all other relationships—and to the people closest in our lives, especially romantic partners and spouses. To understand what shapes our relationships, it is helpful to explore the role models we have inherited from our own parents and our culture. We refer again to the Six Basic Human Needs to illustrate and map how love can be expressed and interpreted in many ways. This understanding supports us in creating meaningful, loving relationships that consider the well-being, needs, and personal growth of everyone involved.

In the second section, we explore the energetics of sexuality. Sexual energy is the most powerful force in our body. If directed downwards through our genital organs, our sexual energy has the potential to create life. If directed upwards, through our system of energy channels and suffused with the virtues of our heart, our sexual energy increases our vitality and assists our process of spiritual awakening. In this section of the module, we explore the energetic principles of sexuality and we learn how to distill sexual energy into spiritual essence through practices of inner alchemy. These techniques can be practiced with or without a partner.

Module 8
"Rediscovering Our Family, Rediscovering Ourselves"

We are all born in a family that presents the exact characteristics we need for our personal development and spiritual growth. Our family, with all its up and downs, good qualities and challenging realities, is the perfect structure to unfold our virtues and test our personal growth and spiritual practice. There is no better spiritual training program than the one our family provides each of us. Nonetheless, to be able to use this spiritual training program without exhausting ourselves, it is vital to have tools to support us in the process.

In this module, first we learn what is the energetic structure of a family. Then, we research the characteristics of our family, the specific reasons why we were born in this family, what we can learn from being part of this family, and, most importantly, how we can be of benefit to this family structure in a profound way that initiates positive, lasting change.

From this positive and appreciative outlook, we consider what are the traumatic generational patterns our family presents—such as abuse, addiction, infertility, divorce, mental illnesses, and suicides. Using the Six Basic Human Needs, we explore how traumatic patterns have affected our families, what the roots of these patterns might be, and how to contribute to the healing of these patterns at the level of the subconscious mind. Finally, to increase and stabilize positive energetic flow through our family, we learn: how to plant the seeds for new healthier patterns for our family's current and future generations; how to strengthen the voice of the inner guide in our family; how to connect our family tree to the finest energies and virtues of Heaven and Earth using the healing sounds of the central channel; and, how to awaken within our present family the spiritual power of our ancestral family through the practice of *Bone Breathing Qi Gong*.

MODULE 9
"DREAM, DEATH, AND TRANSCENDENCE PRACTICES"

This module is divided into two sections: Dream practices and Death and Transcendence practices. Both sections of this module are explored from the understanding that as human beings, our consciousness journeys across four different states of being: the wakeful state, the sleep-dream state, the deep-sleep state, and the all-encompassing state.

In the first section, we explore the potential of our dream and deep sleep states. This is a crucial aspect for us because we spend about one-third of our life sleeping. That is about 25 years sleeping for someone who lives to be 80 years old. Our time sleeping is precious time we can use to restore ourselves and to discover the wonders of our mind.

To help us make the most of our sleeping time, the dream practices explore the importance of balancing our body and energy before falling asleep, how to fall asleep with awareness, and how to use the transitions between waking and sleeping states as daily training to die with a calm, loving, and joyful mind. We also learn how to use our sleep and dream states to promote healing, unfold creativity, and recognize the nature of our awareness.

In the second section, we explore why spiritual practitioners regard death as a celebration where we can attain full and complete awakening. Based on their wisdom, we explore what death is, how to prepare for death, what happens during and after death, what are the different stages of the death process, how sleep and death are related, and how to help the dying and the dead. The purpose of this exploration is to equip us with the understanding and the tools to relate to death with calmness, clarity and joy.

MODULE 10
"SACRED GEOMETRY AND SPACE HARMONIZATION:
THE ART OF THE ANCIENT MASTER BUILDERS"

The spaces we inhabit have a profound influence on our health and well-being. Besides obvious influences like lighting, air circulation, and decoration, spaces influence us due to two main reasons: first, the energetics of the location where the building stands. These energetics include the influences of underground water veins, geological faults, and the energetic meridians of the Earth. And, second, the orientation and proportions of the actual buildings.

Since ancient times, master builders have been aware of the relation between how we feel and the energetic field of the Earth.

This module explores their ancient art to create harmonious spaces that promote health, positive energetic flow, harmonious relationships, enhanced creativity, and spiritual growth. The module is divided in three sections, corresponding to the three levels of harmonization: Earth, Human, and Heaven.

The first section explores the Earth as a living organism, guiding us to experience the energies of underground water veins, geological faults, and Earth's energetic meridians. The second section explores how our human consciousness can impact the energetics of the Earth we explored in the first section. The third section introduces the creation of proportions for building and harmonizing spaces based on the pathway of sun, the moon, and the stars. These three levels of harmonization are the foundation of how temples and sacred sites where developed in the past.

In addition, this module addresses influences on our health that are specific to modern spaces, such as the effects of electricity, wi-fi, cell towers, and electric power lines.

MODULE 11
"PILGRIMAGE AND ENERGETIC JOURNEYS"

This module explores pilgrimage as the spiritual journey a practitioner undergoes to sacred sites after having completed some aspects of her training. Unlike a touristic journey, the practice of pilgrimage is often motivated by an altruistic motivation where we attempt to generate positive energy for the benefit of all beings.

From a traditional point of view, the practice of pilgrimage is a model of how to experience our divine nature and how to approach the death process. The idea of going on pilgrimage is meant to make us reflect on the preciousness of our life and the possibility of death along the way. For this reason, as future pilgrims, we close cycles and resolve pending situations before leaving home.

Traditionally, the practice of pilgrimage is divided into three stages: first, before leaving home we undertake a thorough preparation that might take months or even years; second, once on the actual pilgrimage, we observe certain vows and daily practices that maintain us focused on our purpose and help us connect with the sites we visit; and, third, once we return home, we follow supportive practices that help us integrate our pilgrimage for our benefit and the benefit of others around us.

An alternative to pilgrimage are energetic journeys where we visit sacred sites to experience their energies and learn from the structures left behind by the ancient master builders and spiritual practitioners. Both the practice of pilgrimage and energetic journeys are rich practices that blend our personal healing meditation practice with the traditions of sacred art and the art of the master builders. This module uses the pilgrimage along Saint James trail, across northern Spain, as the model to develop a traditional pilgrimage practice.

MODULE 12
"REMEMBERING THE LIGHT OF OUR HEART"

Remembering the Light of Our Heart is an effortless pilgrimage into the undefinable essence of all things. After having journeyed across the eleven previous modules, we leave behind theories, breathings, visualizations, sounds, movements, and prayers. The practitioner, the practices, and the results of practicing arise together as the spontaneous vibrancy of presence—the heart of all things.

Like a sailor adrift who, after having his senses purified by the winds of grace, realizes that he is the ocean, our natural experience of being spontaneously blossoms from the state of undistracted non-meditation. Witnesses of our consciousness, we experience unadorned self-awareness of being as the practice of all practices, the mantra of all mantras, and the prayer of all prayer. From this full awareness of being, all energies and sounds emanate to create the manifested universe. To this awareness of being everything returns.

Aware that *I am*, through our spontaneous self-awareness, we remember the freedom and joy of our divine identity, the expression of the fullness of the universe as it pulsates from and into itself. In the immediacy of being, here and now, we recall the vastness of who we are, the light at the heart of all things. And, as we heal, we become healers for others. Our being, the essence of all universes, vibrating with one single intention, "May all beings delight in the loving bliss and joy of wakeful being."

BIBLIOGRAPHY

BOOKS

Lao Tsu, Gia-fu Feng, and Jane English. *Tao Te Ching. A New Translation.* New York, Vintage Books, 1997.

Lipton, Bruce. *The Biology of Belief: Unleashing the Power of Consciousness, Matter, & Miracles.* New York, Hay House, 2008.

Maharshi, Ramana. *Atma Bodha.* Bangalore, B.N.Nataraj, 1998.

Matthiessen, Peter. *The Snow Leopard.* New York, Penguin Books, 2018.

Ni, Hua Ching. *Tao: The Subtle Universal Law and the Integral Way of Life.* Los Angeles, Sevenstar Communications, 2003.

Ni, Maoshing. *The Yellow Emperor's Classic of medicine: a new translation of the Neijing Suwen with commentary.* Boston, Shambhala, 1995.

Pert, Candace. *Molecules Of Emotion: The Science Behind Mind-Body Medicine.* New York, Simon and Schuster, 1999.

Rinpoche, Chokyi Nyima. *Sadness, Love, Openness: The Buddhist Path of Joy.* Boston, Shambhala, 2019.

Rinpoche, H.E. Garchen. *Quotes from the Precious One.* Fairfax, Drikung Surya Publications, 2014.

RESEARCH STUDIES AND PAPERS

Brown, Richard P., and Patricia L. Gerbarg. "Yoga Breathing, Meditation, and Longevity." *Annals of the New York Academy of Sciences.* 1172, 2009, 54–62. doi:10.1111/j.1749-6632.2009.04394.x.

Innes, Kim et al. "Mind-body Therapies for Menopausal Symptoms: A Systematic Review." *Maturitas.* 66 2, 2010, 135-49. doi:10.1016/j. maturitas.2010.01.016.

Kahana-Zweig, Roni et al. "Measuring and Characterizing the Human Nasal Cycle." PloS one. 11 10, 2016. doi:10.1371/journal. pone.0162918

Kjellgren, Anette et al. "Wellness through a Comprehensive Yogic Breathing Program. A Controlled Pilot Trial." *BMC Complementary and Alternative Medicine*, 7, 43, 2017. doi:10.1186/1472-6882-7-43

Mariotti, Agnese. "The Effects of Chronic Stress on Health: New Insights into the Molecular Mechanisms of Brain-Body Communication." *Future Science OA* 1 3, 2015. doi:10.4155/fso.15.21

Mehri Bozorg-Nejad et al. "The Effects of Rhythmic Breathing on Pain of Dressing Change in Patients with Burns Referred to Ayatollah Mousavi Hospital." *World Journal of Plastic Surgery*, 7 1, 2018, 51-57.

Puthige, Raghuraj, and Shirley Telles. "Immediate Effect of Specific Nostril Manipulating Yoga Breathing Practices on Autonomic and Respiratory Variables." *Applied Psychophysiology and Biofeedback*. 33, 2008, 65-75. doi:10.1007/s10484-008-9055-0.

Raichle, Marcus E., and Debra A. Gusnard. "Appraising the Brain's Energy Budge." *Proceedings of the National Academy of Sciences of the United States of America*, 99 16, 2002, 10237-10239.

Rani, Khushbu et al. "Six-month Trial of Yoga Nidra in Menstrual Disorder Patients: Effects on Somatoform Symptoms." *Industrial Psychiatry Journal*. 20 2, 2011, 97–102. doi:10.4103/0972-6748.102489

Saxena, Tarun, and Manjari Saxena. "The Effect of Various Breathing Exercises (Pranayama) in Patients with Bronchial Asthma of Mild to Moderate Severity." *International Journal of Yoga*. 2, 2009, 22–25. doi:10.4103/0973-6131.53838.

Sendhilkumar, Ragupathy et al. "Effect of Pranayama and Meditation as an Add-on Therapy in Rehabilitation of Patients with Guillain-Barré Sndrome—a Randomized Control Pilot Study." *Dissability and Rehabilitation*. 35 1. 2013, 57-62.

Werntz, Deborah A. et al. "Alternating Cerebral Hemisphere Activity and the Lateralisation of Autonomic Nervous Function." *Human Neurobiology*. 2, 1983, 39–43

INTERNET RESOURCES:

http://blogs.dailynews.com/friendlyfire/2015/05/23/physics-life-dream/

https://well.blogs.nytimes.com/2011/02/22/cellphone-use-tied-to-changes-in-brain-activity/?searchResultPosition=1

https://www.psychologytoday.com/us/blog/the-happiness-doctor/201706/happiness-and-your-immune-system

https://www.sciencealert.com/99-9999999-of-your-body-is-empty-space

https://www.scientificamerican.com/article/an-hour-of-light-and-sound-a-day-might-keep-alzheimers-at-bay/

ABOUT FERRAN BLASCO-AGUASCA

Ferran Blasco-Aguasca is a practitioner of holistic medicine, with emphasis on Chinese medicine, Biotherapeutic Drainage, and Strategic Intervention coaching. Since graduating in 2005 from Yo San University of Traditional Chinese Medicine, Ferran has been in private practice, guiding people of all ages and walks of life to experience physical, emotional, and mental well-being.

In his clinical practice, Ferran addresses health recovery, well-being maintenance, and personal growth through acupuncture, nutritional support, lifestyle counseling, personal coaching, and healing meditation. Ferran has studied and practiced healing meditation for the last 25 years. *Healing Now* presents his humble understanding of the techniques and key concepts that he finds most useful, both personally and in his clinical practice.

Ferran has led healing meditation workshops and group pilgrimages to sacred sites since 2002. He also conducts regular healing meditation classes at his clinic in Rochester, Michigan, where he lives with his family. Ferran is the founder of the Joyful Heart Institute and the coauthor of *Where Heaven and Earth Unite*, a journey of inquiry into the human heart through the study of sacred sites and the spiritual tradition of the ancient masters builders.

CONTACT

For more information about Ferran Blasco-Aguasca, classes,
coaching and the Joyful Heart Self-Development Program,
you can visit:

www.joyfulheartinstitute.com

Made in the USA
Middletown, DE
24 February 2024

50306671R00146